THE
COLLECTED
Cottage

THE
COLLECTED

Cottage

Gardening, Gatherings, *and* Collecting *at* Chestnut Cottage

KATHRYN CRISP GREELEY

Foreword by JAMES T. FARMER III

Photography by J. WEILAND

GREENLEAF
BOOK GROUP PRESS

Distributed by Greenleaf Book Group

For ordering information or special discounts for bulk purchases,
please contact Greenleaf Book Group at PO Box 91869, Austin, TX 78709, 512.891.6100.

Design and composition by Greenleaf Book Group
Cover design by Greenleaf Book Group
Photographs by J. Weiland

Publisher's Cataloging-in-Publication data is available.

978-1-62634-974-2

Part of the Tree Neutral® program, which offsets the number of trees consumed in the production and
printing of this book by taking proactive steps, such as planting trees in direct proportion to the number of
trees used: www.treeneutral.com

Printed in the United States of America on acid-free paper

22 23 24 25 26 27 28 29   10 9 8 7 6 5 4 3 2 1

First Edition

For Wells

*My best friend, biggest supporter, best cheerleader,
and one who loves Chestnut Cottage as much as I do.*

Thanks for believing in me!

CONTENTS

Foreword

Stepping into Chestnut Cottage, I'm warmly greeted by sensational delights. A welcoming smile and hug from my friends Kathryn "Kathy" and Wells, the scent of popovers rising and turning perfectly golden in the oven, the sight of all my favorite patterns of blue and white porcelain, pottery, and platters, and the sound of Duncan the Westie chirping his bark for me to pet him and scratch behind his ears. Walking into Chestnut Cottage is like walking into my own home with my family. And, my friends, that is the hallmark of true Southern hospitality—feeling completely at home away from home. My dear friends Kathy and Wells invoke and celebrate that hospitality with grace, ease, and elegance! In turn, this elegance and comfort is channeled into Kathy's design work, her books, and special events.

Kathy and I met in the little hamlet of Cashiers, North Carolina, years ago at a Showhouse. We had adjoining spaces—mine a porch off the bedroom she was designing. It was instantaneous friendship. I noticed her monogram. The "K" and the "G" reminding me of Kathryn and Granade—part of my aunt's monogram and spelling "Kathryn" in the same familial spelling. Southerners bond over monograms quite easily! In fact, I told her my Aunt Kathryn has a monogrammed dinnerware company! Kathy

Greeley and I were using mixes of blue and white pottery and porcelain in our spaces, and we bonded over that affinity, too! However, our bond and friendship rooted themselves beyond the aesthetics and acumen of Southern style—we realized that our professional take on creating HOMES, not houses, was paramount to our practice.

Kathryn Greeley Designs is a full-service design firm that creates the types of homes that Kathy and Wells live in as well. From their home in the charming town of Waynesville, North Carolina, to their Chatuge Cottage in Lake Chatuge's spectacular setting, each place is a "welcome home" moment for them, their family, friends, and even those perusing Kathy's books and Instagram. The feeling I get when crossing their threshold is the feeling Kathy's clients receive as they return home. Home tugs at the heartstrings. A house is merely a structure. Home is where we long to be when we're away, where we're at ease, and where we take delight while there. Kathy creates homes for her clients.

From the sumptuous fabrics to the nostalgic notes, Kathy's designs are made for living. Whether in town or country, on the lake or in the mountains, rooms filled with comfortable seating, gorgeous art, and touches of whimsy are the perfect "recipe" for her clients. In the pages ahead, y'all will feel as if you're on a house tour with Kathy! You will be guided page by page to inspiring images filled with all the perfect accoutrements that create a classic home. Kathy's layers in each room invite the client or reader to linger a little longer, enjoy that second cup of coffee, admire the gorgeous dahlias elegantly arranged in just as elegant vases, take in the pitchers and pottery, or simply curl up in a handsome chair with a great read.

My last visit to Chestnut Cottage was the very day fall arrived to the mountains of Western North Carolina. These towns, villages, hamlets, and outposts set within the grandeur of our country's oldest mountains tell a tale of the seasons like no other place on the East Coast. It was summer when I left my home, Joe Pye Cottage, in Cashiers that morning. It felt like a jaunty spring morning by the time we had lunch in the garden, and fall made its debut by that afternoon—with us having tea and dessert on the porch. I love a progressive meal—drinks here, supper there, dessert on the porch—and Kathy provided that for me in her effortless, easy, and elegant way.

Wells Greeley—resident "sommelier" at Chestnut Cottage—is, as I tell him, who I want to be when I grow up. Always the gentleman, dressed handsomely and perfectly mannered like no other, Wells is Kathy's number one fan. He trusts her vision and beams with pride at their delightful home—a testament to her astuteness and design prowess. Fondly reminiscing about dinners past, he showed me some of his favorite menus they have framed in a hallway. Wells toured me around his wine cellar, too, and I learned more and more about his athletic tenure and some first growth vintages, too! A prince of a gent, he is! The ease he and Kathy display in their elegantly appointed home is simply who they are—and a reflection of a life well-lived.

I think of Wells, dressed in tailored threads and always the consummate host, of Kathy in her chic, signature glasses and attire, and I am filled with pride that I know these tasteful, stylish folks. Everything aside, Kathy and Wells Greeley are heartfelt and genuine people I'm even more so blessed to call my friends—true friends and supporters of me and my endeavors. I can count on them for warmth and encouragement, I can "talk shop" about the design business, fuss over hydrangeas and geraniums, and enjoy the places they create and call home—as if these were my own.

For those of us lucky enough to have friends such as these, we are truly lucky enough! Whether it's simple tricks of the trade, learning how to mix strawberry jam and butter for popovers, or being inspired by artwork or art arrangements, Kathy is a delight and considerable joy to know and love. Here, in this new book, I encourage y'all to take a page from her playbook—be inspired to use your silver, invite your friends over for dinner, and celebrate seasons and holidays in Southern style. A lunch at Chestnut Cottage was exactly what I needed upon my last visit. My Mimi, my grandmother, always said, "We eat with our eyes first." And did we ever! From the beautiful flowers to the delicious food, it was truly a visual feast! Mimi also taught me that "we feed people—body and soul—at our tables." This is a legacy I'm proud to uphold—and I'm so thankful for friends like Kathy and Wells who do the same.

I know that your "house tour" with Kathy in this book will feel like a visit with a dear friend. Thank you, Kathy, for taking us all on a tour of your delightful designs. Save me some supper! I'll be "home" with y'all again soon!

James T. Farmer III

Introduction

As I drove up Rolling Drive with my longtime friend and realtor Barbara Henderson, I spotted the cottage. There it was, covered in a lovely blanket of snow, with its emerald-green cedar shakes glowing in the sunlight. At that moment, I knew I was coming home.

To say that I have always felt a deep connection with Chestnut Cottage is a bit of an understatement. On that first visit, the cottage beckoned to me the moment I crossed the threshold. I was drawn in by the warmth and coziness, and I knew it was always meant to be my adult home and quiet retreat. Chestnut Cottage nestles comfortably into the gently rolling landscape and simply has a strong sense of place—a place that has proven to be a collection of the fondest memories of my adult life. As I was an only child, home has always been a special place where I could be myself; nurture and express my hopes, dreams, and personal style; and share the gifts and talents with which I have been blessed.

After months (eighteen, to be exact) of negotiations, on October 2, 1987, I became the proud owner of Chestnut Cottage. As I look back on the transaction, my heart warms to my memory of finally securing it for $72,500. At that time, I was single and a self-employed interior designer, and only by faith and hard work was I able to make my mortgage payments! I knew instinctively that I simply could not fathom ever being without this cottage. It was my empty canvas, both inside and out. However, I did not understand the depth of this strong, almost spiritual attraction that I felt to the cottage at the time I purchased it.

My new neighbors informed me that a lovely couple, Frank and Jesse Miller, had built the home and were the only inhabitants prior to my purchase of it from their son. Every neighbor I spoke with confirmed my suspicion that the previous lady of the house loved this cottage just as I did; it was love at first sight for both of us!

My curiosity about the previous owners led me to make a few further inquiries. Much to my surprise and delight, I learned that Mrs. Miller was from the very same small town as I am—Bryson City, North Carolina! Though seemingly a coincidence, I believe Mrs. Miller's joy and happiness left an imprint on the cottage that complemented my style and encouraged me to mold Chestnut Cottage's current personality. This new personality is built from my own memories, passions, family and friends, and a lifetime of gathering and collecting.

Chestnut Cottage was built in 1924. Mr. Miller was a forester with Champion Paper Company when he decided to build his home on Rolling Drive in Waynesville, North Carolina. For such a lovely home, though, the history of the interior of the cottage begins with the sad story of the American chestnut tree. For several centuries, the American chestnut was a populous tree along the East Coast from Maine to Georgia. This towering hardwood was often referred to as the perfect tree. Many people depended on it for food, lumber, and for their livelihood.

Around 1907, these "perfect trees" were attacked by the chestnut blight, which originated in Asia. It is believed that in 1904, a forester from the Bronx Zoo brought in Asian chestnut trees to decorate his homestead. Billions of American chestnuts were destroyed, and the tree faced extinction. At that time, dead chestnut trees were being dragged out of the forests of Western North Carolina and were considered junk wood. It would be my guess that Mr. Miller had access to this so-called junk wood and decided to finish the interior of his home with what is now commonly referred to as "wormy chestnut."

Chestnut Cottage is enveloped in this unique wood—ceilings, walls, windows, trim, and doors, which are three-boards thick. As I wandered through the cottage on my first visit, I noted that no two boards were the same—not in width, in grain, nor in "worm holes." What else struck me was the sad condition of the wood, darkened by years of cigarette smoke. With a vision and the will not to be deterred, I knew my work would begin with gallons of Murphy Oil Soap!

My second task upon arrival at Chestnut Cottage (after weeks of washing the chestnut from top to bottom to remove the black smoke damage) was to paint the entire kitchen white. With medium-stained oak floors, a classic white kitchen appealed to my design aesthetic and made for a nice contrast with the warm chestnut wood. I should also note that it would seem that Mr. Miller ran short of chestnut when it was time to finish the walls and ceilings, as tongue and groove pine was used to finish the kitchen ceiling, walls, and trim. Thus, there's a mix of three woods in this space.

Happily, the sad story of the American chestnut has a hopeful ending thanks to a chestnut restoration program and The American Chestnut Foundation. The foundation is exploring a number of promising avenues to repopulate this mighty tree. Their goal is to develop a blight-resistant American chestnut tree through scientific research and breeding. My husband and I are members of the foundation and now have a chestnut seedling at Chestnut Cottage. In his 1936 poem "Evil Tendencies Cancel," Robert Frost mused about the future of the mighty American chestnut.

> *"Will the blight end the chestnut?*
> *The farmers rather guess not.*
> *It keeps smouldering at the roots*
> *And sending up new shoots*
> *Till another parasite*
> *Shall come to end the blight."*

For six years, I worked like a woman possessed to create the cottage of my dreams. This "empty canvas" was the perfect motivation for me to cultivate my collecting desires. My mother often referred to my collecting as an addiction, but I prefer to call it my passion. I had begun collecting blue and white wares years earlier and had acquired several treasured pieces of antique furniture.

My blue and white collection was a perfect starting point for a color scheme that remains today—even after several additions and alterations to the cottage. English chintz combined with English and Irish antiques began to appear at Chestnut Cottage, and years of hunting and gathering would slowly mold the personality of this cozy cottage.

In 1993, Wells Greeley and I were married at Chestnut Cottage with family and a few friends in attendance. Shortly after our wedding, Wells and I determined we would need to add space to the cottage, as he had two children who would live part-time with us. Two small bedrooms and one small bathroom would not do.

"Be not forgetful to entertain strangers:
for thereby some have entertained
angels unaware."

—HEBREWS 13:2

I immediately knew we needed to consult my office partner at that time, Randy Cunningham. Randy was a talented architect, whom I trusted to make an addition that would look as if it had always been part of this special cottage. He did not disappoint, and neither did my friend Ron Leatherwood, who was and continues to be the "contractor of record"! The renovation resulted in an enlarged kitchen and a master bedroom suite. Who would have ever imagined that "junk wood" would be so highly coveted, expensive, and hard to find years later? But not continuing with wormy chestnut was never a consideration. So, we went about sourcing this "perfect wood" to make the addition look as if it had always belonged.

Several years later, on a trip to England and Ireland, I visited many houses, large and small, with wonderful glass conservatories. Once back home, I decided Chestnut Cottage must have a conservatory too. But after a couple of British companies provided proposals that were at least four times the original cost of the cottage, I decided that Chestnut Cottage indeed did *not* need a conservatory! Instead, work began on plans to enclose our existing patio, which was open to both the kitchen and the master bedroom. This room would become our "keeping room," with a seating area with a fireplace, space for a baby grand piano, and a dining table for eight. This new room allowed for two very important items: more space for collections and more space for entertaining, both of which are passions for me!

Wells generously offered to build a new house. My response was that such a project would end in a swift divorce, as I never intended to leave my cottage!

Collected, Not Decorated

I believe my passion for collecting is rooted in my love of history. When I purchase a piece, particularly an antique, I pause to consider the history of the item—the skill of the craftsman who made it, the places it has "lived" prior to my purchase, and simply its beauty. I look at collecting in two distinct ways: the beauty of the piece in and of itself and its purpose. My collections have definitely inspired my passion for entertaining, since I feel the opportunity to share the beauty of a collection is certainly a reason to plan memorable and beautiful entertaining events.

I inherited my passion for entertaining from my mother, who believed, as I do, that entertaining is a gift to family, friends, and strangers alike. In my forty-year design career, I have always encouraged clients to collect items that speak to them: items they find on their travels and items they would use in their own particular lifestyles. I like to work with pieces that clients have collected because I feel our collections tell the stories of our lives and what is important to us. As an interior designer, I place great value on creating lifestyles, as well as simply designing interiors. I wanted Chestnut Cottage to have a sense of history. Had I not been an interior design major, I would have been a history major.

> # Anything that you love is always a good choice.

I prefer a room to look as if it has evolved over time, while continuing to look fresh. You could say I like layers of historical charm in a room, since they seem to give the room a depth of character. I feel each piece should tell a story or evoke a memory, and that is what collecting can achieve. For many years, my mantra has been to design rooms that are "collected, not decorated."

I also feel rooms should reflect the owners' personalities. I wanted Chestnut Cottage to be elegant, casual, approachable, comfortable, and thoughtful. After all, the rooms we design set a stage on which we live our lives. My vision was for Chestnut Cottage to exude warmth and welcome.

Through the years, I have done a great deal of editing and refining at Chestnut Cottage. It is and will continue to be a work in progress. I don't think a home is ever "done." Our collections become part of our story and our memories as we continue to refine. Therefore, I recommend collecting things that build your story, rather than items that just function as furnishings. Each piece has a story to tell, whether that piece was inherited or sourced from an antique dealer.

I believe people are far happier when their homes are unique to them and reflect who they are. My collections of china, crystal, and silver are numerous, and I use these collections daily. And all of my other collections are used as part of the overall design of Chestnut Cottage. They also are set out—rather than stored in cupboards—to be enjoyed and used in daily service.

The First Big Party at the Cottage

As I mentioned, when I purchased Chestnut Cottage, I was single, and 935 square feet suited my lifestyle—even my early entertaining needs. My first big party at the cottage was a black-tie event given with my friend James Roy Moody. James Roy and I were soulmates, and our friendship lasted many years until his death. His passing could never rob me of all the precious memories we shared, many of which include us entertaining together at Chestnut Cottage. As a matter of fact, James Roy introduced me to Wells! "JR" and I couldn't even get through one event before we started planning the next.

But back to our first big party together. As Chestnut Cottage was a tiny venue for entertaining, I was initially concerned about the space, but JR convinced me that we would keep the invitation list small, and space would absolutely not be a problem. We spent months planning the details. First, we decided it was going to be black-tie. Perhaps, we thought, this would deter some of the people on our guest list, which was growing significantly each day. We then decided our invitation should be written in French (that, too, we thought, would reduce the number of guests!). We ended up loving all the chaos this caused, with people running all over town trying to get their invitations translated, since JR and I had agreed that neither of us would translate the invitation for *anyone*! Before we knew it, we had sent out over 150 invitations.

Soon I was worrying day and night about how many guests I could fit into Chestnut Cottage. I hoped and prayed that the dress code and the invitation in French would give us less than fifty people. But my prayers were not answered. Our "inclusive natures" seemed to be working against us. Nevertheless, the show had to go on! Beautiful food had to be prepared, and the cottage had to be dressed in its best holiday finery.

On the night of the party, it was equally horrifying and glorious to see over 100 of our close friends arrive all decked out for the occasion. Cars were parked up and down the street and in neighbors' driveways. There was simply no place to put all these people. But at this point, we had no choice but to get on with it! I will note it was gratifying to see that, amazingly, every guest had followed the dress code to the letter. That is . . . all but one. He was wearing a black tie, for sure—but that was ALL! (That's another story that probably wouldn't make the cut with my publisher!) This event with JR ended up adding even more fuel to my ongoing passion for entertaining at Chestnut Cottage. Large and small groups now gather here regularly for all sorts of events.

The recent pandemic has served to remind us that we must savor the small joys of our lives. We must embrace our passions, not simply in the momentous events in life, but in all of our daily happenings. Each of us have that creative ability and force within us, if only we cultivate it!

The Garden of My Dreams

Not only was the interior of the cottage my empty canvas. So were the grounds surrounding it, and they would become the garden of my dreams. From my many visits to England, Ireland, and Scotland, I developed a great affection for the cottage garden style. What springs to mind when you think of a cottage garden? For me, it is a small plot, with a jumble

CHESTNUT COTTAGE

of flowers—hollyhocks, foxgloves, lilacs, scented roses, delphiniums, lupines, sweet peas, and, of course, peonies!

My vision also included boxwood hedges and topiaries, herbs for the kitchen, stone paths leading to secret places, and a spring profusion of daffodils, tulips, and forsythia. The garden had to be cozy and informal, with the flowers as the stars—flowers that would fill the cottage with arrangements for most of the year. The giant old oak trees surrounding the cottage would provide an array of autumn colors, and orange, gold, and yellow dahlias would add even more. And I envisioned pine, and holly, and the scarlet red of the winter-berries. Finally, there would be a gate leading to the back door, where the scent of 'New Dawn' roses would welcome everyone to the cottage.

A cottage garden, just like your home, evolves over time, as has the garden at Chestnut Cottage. English-style cottages and gardens evoke a sense of timeless romance for me. I think the views outside your home and your connection to nature bring great joy. Another blessing the garden has gifted me is patience—which is really not in my nature!

Come with Me

Come with me, and be my guest at Chestnut Cottage . . . *The Collected Cottage*. One of the joys of living in Western North Carolina is that we have four distinct seasons. Later in the book, we'll also take a little journey to Chatuge Cottage, our lake house, for a peek at more collections and a birthday party for one of my favorite gentlemen in history. But for now, your year-long visit will begin with spring, which is perhaps my favorite season at the cottage because the garden is truly in its glory, and it makes for a perfect time to entertain!

It is my hope that this book will inspire you to create your own warm, welcoming sanctuary—a place to create memories, entertain family and friends, collect, and find the joys of nature.

"Therefore all seasons shall be sweet to thee."

—SAMUEL TAYLOR COLERIDGE

Spring

*"Spring makes its own statement,
so loud and clear that the gardener seems to be only
one of his instruments, not the composer."*

—GEOFFREY B. CHARLESWORTH

Daffodils

I wandered lonely as a cloud
That floats on high o'er vales and hills,
When all at once I saw a crowd,
A host, of golden daffodils;
Beside the lake, beneath the trees,
Fluttering and dancing in the breeze.

Continuous as the stars that shine
And twinkle on the Milky Way,
They stretched in never-ending line
Along the margin of a bay:
Ten thousand saw I at a glance,
Tossing their heads in sprightly dance.

The waves beside them danced; but they
Out-did the sparkling waves in glee:
A poet could not but be gay
In such a jocund company:
I gazed—and gazed—but little thought
What wealth the show to me had brought:

For oft, when on my couch I lie
In vacant or in pensive mood,
They flash upon that inward eye
Which is the bliss of solitude,
And then my heart with pleasure fills
And dances with the daffodils.

—WILLIAM WORDSWORTH
(1770–1850)

In the Garden

S pring brings my two favorite flowers—first, the daffodils, and later, the peonies. It is a blooming succession that you hope will continue on for weeks once it commences. The winter's snow has left us, and a delicate spring rain begins to fall upon the Chestnut Cottage garden. The brave hellebore flowers may wilt in the last of the severe frosts, but they pick themselves back up—and stand, heads nodding, through the rest of the bad weather. The warm sun awakens a profusion of sleeping spring bulbs, and still the hellebores continue to parade their delicate colors, with the real showoff being the 'New York Nights' with its shades of black! The soft pink petals of the cherry tree flowers emerge, and the sparrows begin to sing.

The hellebores are still blooming when the snowdrops make their first appearance. I am intrigued by the delicate form of the snowdrops as well as their exquisite coloring. The variety at Chestnut Cottage is actually referred to as a *snowflake*, Leucojum aestivm 'Gravetye Giants.' Snowdrops are often called the surest sign of spring. As delicate as these flowers appear, they often push their way up through the snow.

At the first sight of the snowdrops, I know the daffodils will be coming soon. When my birthday rolls around in early March, I'm blessed with numerous varieties to fill up the cottage. Then come the tulips! And right after that, suddenly it's Easter and time for our annual Easter lunch for family and friends. With spring comes my strong desire to garden, entertain, arrange flowers, and visit nurseries and plant festivals.

I truly feel spring is in the air!

Once the ground begins to warm and the spring sun bathes the garden, the daffodils burst forth. Recently, we planted 2,600 new daffodils and tulips. My favorites are 'Sailorman,' 'Pistachio,' 'Dancing Moonlight,' 'Ice Follies,' 'Precocious,' 'Cassida,' 'Obdam,' and 'Zaragoza.' Other varieties in the garden include 'Happy Smiles,' 'Congress,' 'Flower Parade,' and 'Orange Sunset.'

While the daffodils are still blooming, along come the double tulips and some white parrot tulips. We are trying two new varieties of double tulips this year. 'Foxtrot' has a pink to deep-pink color at the base that moves up the petals to join a lighter pink decorated with white and green highlights. 'Marie Jo' has a lushly layered bloom with a slightly ruffled edge. It is a brilliant sunshine-yellow with a soft fragrance.

Did you know that daffodils are safe from rabbits because they contain a poisonous substance called lycorine? Inter-planting tulips among these "unsavory options" is helpful in deterring the bunnies from lunching on our tulips! With daffodils still putting on their show, peonies, foxgloves, lupines, forget-me-nots, and grape hyacinths are also popping up in the garden. As if anyone could ask for more, all of this beauty is framed in the loveliest border of cherry trees that provide a soft, pink canopy.

Of course, to make this magic happen, there are many spring garden chores that must be done! Before we get the daffodils all "tied down," it is time to do the window boxes and containers.

Duncan MacDuff is always helpful in my constant effort to keep the cottage filled with the different varieties of daffodils and tulips, as long as they are blooming.

EARLY–MID SPRING GARDEN CHORES

Aerate the lawn and mulch the beds with leaf compost.

Start weeding to stay on top of this never-ending job!

Plant new perennials and annuals after
the threat of frost has passed.

Start staking plants that need support, such
as peonies, delphiniums, and false indigo.

Fertilize all plants.

Prune and fertilize roses.

Plant window boxes and containers.

LATE SPRING GARDEN CHORES

Trim all topiaries.

Tie down bulbs.

"Chelsea Chop."

I have very definite ideas about what I want in the window boxes, which means I reserve my plants early at several local nurseries. Most of our boxes and containers are in the sun, but a few must be planted with shade plants. Over the years, I have experimented with different plants, and I always use those that thrive and suit me best from a design point of view. My sun boxes and containers contain 'Calliope Burgundy' Geraniums, Scented Heliotrope, Dark Purple Petunias, 'Lemon Slice' Calibrachoa, 'Blue Eyes' Lobelia, Alyssum, Angelonia, and Bacopa. My shade boxes and containers hold white New Guinea Impatiens, 'Gingerland' Caladiums, 'Kimberly Queen' Fern, ivy, 'Non-Stop Red' Begonias, and fuchsia.

In May, just in time for Mother's Day, the garden begins to transition from early spring bloomers to borders that are overflowing with peonies, foxgloves, delphiniums, lupines, and all of my cottage favorites.

Of these, it's the peonies I look forward to most!

The garden at Chestnut Cottage is truly one of my greatest joys, and I wait patiently all year for it to put on a show. The peony collection includes 'Sarah Bernhardt'—which is, perhaps, my favorite—along with 'Reine Hortense,' 'Duchesse de Nemours,' 'Shawnee Chief,' 'Monsieur Jules Elie,' 'Bowl of Beauty,' 'Vivid Rose,' 'Dr. Alexander Fleming,' and 'Festiva Maxima.'

I enjoy peonies in the garden, but I simply can't resist bringing them indoors for lots of arrangements. The soft pink of the 'Sarah Bernhardt' is such a lovely contrast with the cobalt in my Flow Blue vases and containers.

Where daffodils and tulips were in bloom only a month ago, now the garden delivers not only several varieties of peonies, but also several varieties of foxgloves. The form of each of the foxgloves is so intricate, and that is a testament to the fact that no one designs quite like nature! We have plenty of *Digitalis* 'Foxy,' *Digitalis* 'Dalmatian Purple,' and the rather unusual variety, *Digitalis* 'Pam's Split.' I love the way the foxgloves manage to reseed them-selves each year in the most random of places.

The late spring garden seems to have a perfect color palette of pinks, blues, and purples. The deep blue of the 'Magic Fountain Dark Blue/White Bee' delphinium, and the deep blue of the Baptisia 'Sparkling Sapphire,' which is commonly known as False Indigo, are brilliant against the purple and pink lupines.

The delicate blue of the Nigella Damascena or Love-in-a-Mist brings a different texture to the array of blues in the borders. I enjoy the different shades of pink and soft red in the bi-color blooms of the *Dianthus Barbatus* or 'Indian Carpet' Sweet Williams.

The garden also has *Baptisia* 'Pink Truffles' to add to the pink palette. Many years ago, I planted *Iris Pseudacoru*, also known as 'Yellow Flag' iris, to add a pop of yellow to the pinks, blues, and purples.

At this time in the garden, the deep-rose rhododendron begins to fade just as the beautiful *Rhododendron Calendulaceum*, commonly known as flame azalea, and the *Kalmia Latifolia*, commonly known as mountain laurel, start to bloom.

The *Alchemilla Mollis* or Lady's Mantle spills over most of the borders and seems to hold drops of dew most of the day. Not only is it a perfect edge for the borders, but it is also a perfect texture in floral arrangements.

We have several old 'Very Berry' rhododendron plants that can be spotted in the borders.

With all this beauty in the garden, I could be tempted to "rest on my laurels." But, no,

there is still much work to be done! For example, the very time-consuming job of "tying down" the daffodils.

To avoid interrupting the food manufacturing process of the plants, the foliage of daffodils cannot be cut until it is yellowed and withered, after the blooms have faded. You can choose an uncomplicated tie-down method that will hide any unsightly foliage in the garden, and while this requires setting aside some time, it makes for a much tidier spring garden.

Of course, that's not the only chore. I'm referring to the "Chelsea Chop," so called because it is usually carried out at the end of May, coinciding with the Royal Horticulture Society (RHS) Chelsea Flower Show. The Chelsea Chop is a pruning method by which you limit the size and control the flowering season of many herbaceous plants. Our box-wood hedges and topiaries must also be trimmed and given a fresh edge.

We have all sizes and shapes of topiaries in the garden, but one that is very close to my heart was given to me by a dear friend who helped me design the Chestnut Cottage garden. Hunter Stubbs, who sadly passed away at the young age of forty-two, made a West Highland Terrier form and planted a boxwood under it in memory of our first Westie, Bentley Greeley. This little topiary stands watch over the back garden borders. Hunter knew how impatient I am and warned me that "Bentley" would take some time to fill in. He was indeed right, but now the little Westie is almost completely full! The imprint

of Hunter's creativity and horticultural knowledge remains evident in my garden, and I greatly miss his sense of humor about gardening.

I, too, can keep watch over the back garden while I relax on the old stone bench above the "Bentley" topiary.

Because the land at the back of the cottage slopes toward it, we have had an ongoing challenge with water runoff. A few years ago, we installed French drains on the entire lower borders. I like borders to tightly meet the turf, but sadly the French drains don't allow for that, so the drains are covered with a combination of river rock, leaf mold, and triple ground mulch. At any rate, I certainly prefer plants spilling over the turf rather than water sneaking into the cottage!

By this time, the hard frosts and chilly weather are hopefully over, and it's time to start entertaining outdoors. The courtyard at the back door provides a cozy, private space for a small luncheon for a few friends.

In late spring, the rose garden begins to come into its own and ushers in another collection of blooms—and ideas for entertaining guests. This time of year, my David Austin rose plantings give off a mix of heavenly scents. My favorite in the front garden is called 'Teasing Georgia.'

This free-flowering climber produces blooms into the fall, each with a rich yellow center that fades to the palest yellow on the edges. Another of my favorites in this collection is 'Tess of the D'Urbervilles.' Named after the heroine of Thomas Hardy's novel, this rose is a climber, bearing large, deeply cupped, bright-crimson blooms with a lovely Old Rose fragrance.

My favorite pink rose in the garden is 'The Ancient Mariner,' again from David Austin. Its many large-petal blooms have a lovely, glowing, mid-color pink at the center that pales towards the edges. Over time, the blooms reveal clusters of golden stamens. Also in the front garden are the 'Claire Austin' roses, whose cupped, pale-lemon buds open to a large, creamy-white flower. The outer petals are perfectly arranged in concentric circles, often with a touch of pink.

Our front topiary garden is a combination of *Buxus sempervirens* shapes, along with two "cloud" groupings of Ilex crenata 'Compacta' and several varieties of ferns, hostas, and Tiarclla.

Each year, we try to add one or two topiaries, and this area is finally filling in to give a nice, deep-green color that contrasts with the boulder wall. Sadly, the espaliered apple trees were nipped by a late frost and did not bear any apples this year. But, even without fruit, they soften the high rock wall of the front porch. It seems that the front garden is saying, "I am ready for more outdoor entertaining."

Gatherings

Easter Luncheon

E ach year at Easter, we invite a fairly sizeable number of family and friends to join us for lunch. We have anywhere from twelve to thirty guests, depending on who is in town for the holiday. Much like our Thanksgiving meal, the Easter menu rarely varies. My guests tell me they would be very disappointed if I deviated from it.

Easter Luncheon Menu

Baked Ham

Rosemary Grilled Baby Lamb Chops

Margaret's Potato Salad

Deviled Eggs

Green Beans

Broccoli Bake

Pineapple Casserole

Chilled Asparagus in Walnut Vinaigrette

Pinch Bread

Easy Coconut Cake

Individual Lemon Tarts

Table Inspiration

Perhaps due to the blooming garden, Easter always makes me think of pastels. Because of this, it's no surprise that it is my custom to use my favorite china pattern to set the stage for the lunch. You may remember this pattern from my first book, *The Collected Tabletop*. "Old Coalport" by Coalport China just says "*happy spring*" to me!

Many years ago, I fell in love with this pattern, featuring triple cobalt borders, gold leaf, and the bright color palette of unique floral sprays. Many of the flowers depicted in this pattern bloom in the Chestnut Cottage garden. The pieces are marked with "Old Coalport Period 1825" and "Made in England." This pattern was reproduced by Coalport China between 1979 and 1983 under the pattern name "Leighton Spray." Researching their listings indicates that Coalport China has several floral patterns called "Old Coalport." My collection is designated "Old Coalport (Gold Trim)." To add a bit of a mystery, I often refer to this lovely pattern simply as "Leighton Spray." That just sounds more elegant than "Old Coalport"!

Another favorite element on the Easter table is my vintage cobalt egg cups. I found one years ago at an antique shop and never stopped looking for more. Then miraculously, on my birthday one year, my good friend and antiquing buddy Holli Morris presented me with seven more of these delightful little bunnies, each holding an egg cup. To add a hint of new, I found some whimsical bronze rabbits while at a furniture market and use them on one of the tables. I fill their little baskets with pastel-colored Médicis Jordan Almonds from Paris.

Several years ago, I engaged Leslie McCullough of LTM Designs to design a custom monogram for Chestnut Cottage. Leslie often does custom place cards, menu cards, and even invitations with this lovely monogram for me. For Easter, she has done all three, with beautiful cobalt papers picking up the border in the china pattern. I asked her to do custom notepads as my Easter favors for guests, and then I added a fun white and gold bamboo pen.

I was so taken with this monogram design I even went so far as to have Leontine Linens elegantly interpret it on their linen napkins. As an incurable collector, I simply can't resist beautiful linens. Many years ago, I found an exquisite set of napkins and a tablecloth in London, and for Easter, I mix this antique tablecloth with the crisp new Leontine napkins. The details of the tablecloth—the embroidery and the open fabric work—bring a sense of history to the table.

A mix of cobalt and clear Saint Louis "Tommy" crystal adds the necessary sparkle to the table.

No table at Chestnut Cottage would ever be complete without flowers—lots of flowers! The spring garden is most generous with its offerings, and I add in other favorite seasonal blossoms from the floral wholesaler. The bright-yellow daffodils and double tulips bring perpetual sunshine inside the cottage.

One of the main reasons I grow tulips is to see them in my tulipiere! Tulipieres first came to prominence during the tulip-trading mania in Holland in the 1600s. These elaborate tulip vessels were most often created in the quintessentially Dutch blue and white pottery called Delftware. Originally designed to sprout bulbs, my tulipieres function as vases that provide a forum for the glorious tulip, and they delight gardeners of all persuasions. Sometimes I use the tulipiere for other flowers, but in the spring, it is reserved for our tulips!

I find great joy in flower arranging but must admit that I don't follow the "rules of arranging." I suppose over the years I have developed my own style of arranging flowers, and the garden at the cottage has certainly aided in that development. I have one little closet stuffed with vases and containers. I love using a variety of vintage flower "frogs," floral foam, and clear tape, and it's serendipitous that my passion for collecting extends to containers in which I can arrange flowers. I never visit an antique shop without looking around for potential flower containers. I think this is because flowers simply inspire me and bring me joy!

I bring out a variety of silver vases for spring blooms during Easter entertaining, as well as a collection of cobalt beehive vases to hold several varieties of daffodils.

On any given spring morning, I can't wait to get my trug off the back porch and head to the garden. Then, it's back to the "vase closet" to select the perfect vessel for my harvest. If you are reading this and thinking to yourself, *I can't arrange flowers because I don't have a garden*, then I say, "*No excuses!*" Local grocery stores and flower markets have a variety of lovely blooms. Joy is waiting for you, too!

Chestnut Cottage

Menu

BAKED HAM
ROSEMARY GRILLED BABY LAMB CHOPS

~

MARGARET'S POTATO SALAD
DEVILED EGGS
GREEN BEANS
BROCCOLI BAKE
PINEAPPLE CASSEROLE
CHILLED ASPARAGUS IN WALNUT VINAIGRETTE

~

PINCH BREAD

~

EASY COCONUT CAKE
INDIVIDUAL LEMON PIE TARTS

As you know, my Easter menu is always the same, and it is an extensive one, as I try to include everyone's favorites.

Two of my own menu choices are our Rosemary Grilled Baby Lamb Chops and my Easy Coconut Cake. My most cherished recipes seem to always come from family and friends. The Easy Coconut Cake recipe is no exception; it's from my friend and client Vicki West. I typically make it on the Friday or Saturday before Easter and keep it in our wine cellar or the refrigerator. It is so moist, and I think you will find it surprisingly easy to make. This cake was one of my mother's favorites, and I think of her and miss her every time I make it.

I always bake a whole ham to go along with the grilled lamb chops. Years ago, I started playing around with a marinade recipe for the lamb, and I finally settled on this easy rosemary and citrus combination. These meats are the headliners for all the other guest favorites, and I follow everything with the Easy Coconut Cake and individual lemon tarts.

Easy Coconut Cake

INGREDIENTS

For the Cake

1 white pudding-in-the-mix cake mix
Fresh eggs and vegetable oil to add to
the mix

I use Betty Crocker Super Moist White Cake Mix with pudding in the mix.

For the Sour Cream Filling

16 ounces sour cream
12 ounces shredded coconut, thawed if
previously frozen
2 cups granulated sugar

Note: You will set aside ½ cup of this filling to be used in the Whipped Cream Frosting to frost the outside and top of the cake.

For the Whipped Cream Frosting

3 cups heavy whipping cream
5 tablespoons Marshmallow Fluff
5 tablespoons confectioner's sugar
2 teaspoons pure vanilla extract

PREPARATION

The Cake

Prepare the cake mix according to package directions and pour batter into two 8-inch round cake pans. Cook according to package directions. Remove the two cakes from the oven and cool on a cooling rack. When cakes are cool, slice each horizontally to make a total of four cake layers.

The Sour Cream Filling

Combine sour cream, coconut, and sugar in a small bowl. Blend well with a spoon. Reserve ½ cup of this mixture in a separate bowl to use in the frosting and place both bowls in the refrigerator to chill.

The Whipped Cream Frosting

Note: Chill whipping cream, mixing bowl, and beaters before starting the frosting. A stainless-steel bowl is the best choice for whipping cream.

Melt the Marshmallow Fluff in the microwave for 5-second intervals until just melted. Stir gently until slightly cooled and thick and gooey. In the bowl of a stand mixer fitted with a whisk attachment (or you can use a hand mixer), beat the whipping cream until soft peaks form. Stir the melted Marshmallow Fluff into the whipped cream and slowly stir in the confectioner's sugar and vanilla extract. Beat on high speed until stiff peaks form.

ASSEMBLING THE CAKE

Spread all but ½ cup of sour cream filling on each of three layers of the cake. Stack each layer on the next, then the final cake layer on the very top. Add the reserved ½ cup of the sour cream filling to the prepared whipped cream frosting. Mix well and spread on the top and sides of the cake. Place in the refrigerator until ready to serve.

Rosemary Grilled Baby Lamb Chops

INGREDIENTS

12 single baby rib lamb chops, Frenched
  (about 2 to 2½ pounds)

½ cup extra-virgin olive oil

2 tablespoons garlic, minced

2 tablespoons fresh rosemary leaves, minced

2 tablespoons fresh mint leaves, minced

4 tablespoons fresh-squeezed orange juice

1 teaspoon salt

2 teaspoons orange zest

1 teaspoon ground black pepper

PREPARATION

Place the lamb chops in a baking dish. In a bowl, combine the oil, garlic, rosemary, mint, orange juice, salt, orange zest, and pepper. Pour marinade over the chops and turn to coat both sides. Refrigerate for at least four hours.

Preheat grill to medium-high. Place the lamb chops on the grill and cook, turning once during the cooking process, about 2 to 3 minutes per side for medium-rare.

Remove the chops from the grill and serve with mint jelly. I use Rosebud Farms Mint Jelly from the UK. Of course, a homemade version would be delightful!

Note: For our Easter lunch, I usually triple this recipe, and so I use a large plastic bag to hold the marinade and turn the bag several times as the chops are marinating.

We all know how tiring entertaining events can be, but certain small things end up making them all worthwhile. I believe entertaining our family and friends is our gift *to* them. The gifts we get back in return *from* them come in the observations that warm our hearts and create memories that time can never take from us. For me, these include seeing Duncan waiting under the feet of the person carving the ham in great hopes that a few juicy bites will come his way and a dear cousin who always savors every detail of my flower arrangements.

After the last dishes are washed, the crystal is dried, and the silver is put up, I pour myself a glass of champagne or a cup of tea and ponder the day's events, which always include lots of smiles and gratitude from our wonderful guests. Each guest makes me feel that they truly appreciate my efforts, and that they are looking forward to our next meal together.

Honoring Our Mothers

"To plant a garden is to believe in tomorrow."

—AUDREY HEPBURN

Honoring Our Mothers Menu

Brut Rosé Champagne

Chilled Rosé and Strawberry Soup

Margaret's Hot Chicken Salad

Tomato Aspic

Classic Popovers with Strawberry Butter

Blueberry Goat Cheese Tart

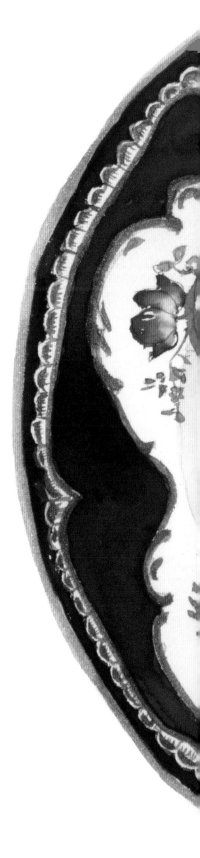

I was extremely close to my mother, and through the years, I have become close with many of my friends' mothers. So, I thought a lovely spring luncheon to honor our mothers would be a perfect way to start the outdoor entertaining season. As a side note, let me say right now that there is nothing more valuable than a sturdy, sixty-inch, round, folding table, if you enjoy setting a table to entertain—particularly outdoors.

Table Inspiration

The sweet smell and breathtaking blooms of the 'New Dawn' roses and peonies provided the perfect inspiration for my design of the Mother's Day luncheon table. Mother's Day seems to put me in a soft-pink state of mind. I had a fabric of large pink and white checks from Old World Weavers made into a round tablecloth, and from that point, the tone was "think pink."

When Wells and I married, several friends gave us a lovely china pattern, "Charlotte" by Royal Worcester, which was established in 1751. Its cobalt and gold border with a cobalt lattice pattern is paired with pastel floral bouquets, making it a perfect complement to the garden's perennial borders. Royal Worcester is believed to be the oldest or second-oldest English porcelain brand still in existence today. I say "or second-oldest" because this is disputed by Royal Crown Derby, which claims 1750 is the year of their establishment. Regardless of the dispute, I find great joy in my patterns from both of these companies, which you will discover in this book.

Frequent trips to antique shops and shows inspire many of my tabletop designs and concepts for events. I purchased these Italian Murano glass bowls with an under plate from an antique dealer who explained that the darker pieces of glass on the outside of these pieces were "shot" onto the outside surface of each piece. I thought the combination of texture and the slight difference in the pink color made these bowls very interesting and perfect for my Chilled Rose and Strawberry Soup.

My very first crystal pattern was "Lismore" by Waterford. I enjoy mixing it with "Colleen," so a brut rosé was served in "Colleen" champagne flutes on this special occasion. My mother had a strong preference for Waterford crystal. Perhaps that was because her father was from County Down in Northern Ireland, and she felt a deep loyalty to the Emerald Isle.

I added some small pink antique juice glasses with an elegant grape leaf design, which gave a pop of color and were perfect for serving a glass of wine for those who wanted something in addition to the rosé.

I also thought it would be appropriate to use Mother's wedding silver flatware, which is "Processional" by Fine Arts.

The simplicity of this pattern mixes nicely with the more intricate design in the china. Monogrammed napkins from Leontine Linens pulled out the shades of pink in the china and the tablecloth, and a bit of blue tied into the cobalt in the china pattern.

I transformed a silver English "trophy bowl" into the perfect container for peonies, roses, Sweet Williams, and the touch of blue found in the delicate Love-in-a-Mist blooms from the garden. One of our favorite David Austin roses is the lovely pink, scented 'Miranda,' which I felt compelled to add. When I am arranging flowers from the garden, I seem to keep going back for just one more thing, such as pink cosmos in this particular arrangement! Think pink, right?

My mother was known for her Hot Chicken Salad recipe. If someone was sick, she took them some, and if there was a death in a family, she prepared it. Anytime she was asked to bring a dish, she turned to Hot Chicken Salad. It even became so popular with my employees that someone always brought it for birthday lunches at the office! It's a staple in my recipe files and is perfect as an individual serving or in a casserole for a crowd.

Margaret's Hot Chicken Salad

INGREDIENTS

4 cups cooked and shredded
    chicken breasts

1 cup diced celery

⅓ cup diced white onion

1 10½-ounce can of cream of
    mushroom soup

1 cup Duke's Mayonnaise*

2 cups grated mild cheddar, divided
    (reserve 1 cup for topping)

½ cup toasted, slivered almonds

1 8-ounce bag of Lays Classic Potato
    Chips*, roughly crushed

PAM cooking spray (or 1–2 table-
    spoons vegetable oil for greasing the
    baking dish)*

Note: I usually cook my chicken the day before in the Crock Pot with chicken broth and a couple of cloves of garlic.

*You can substitute your favorite brands of mayonnaise, potato chips, and cooking spray.

PREPARATION

Preheat oven to 425 degrees.

Mix the first seven ingredients together (reserving 1 cup of the cheese) and spread into a 9x13-inch baking dish that has been greased or sprayed with PAM cooking spray. Top mixture with remaining grated cheese and the crushed potato chips. Bake for 30 minutes.

For a more festive effect, bake in individual ramekins!

Menu

Brut Rosé Champagne

Chilled Rosé & Strawberry Soup

Margaret's Hot Chicken Salad

Tomato Aspic

Classic Popovers with Strawberry Butter

Blueberry Goat Cheeze Tart

When I was thinking about this luncheon menu, I chuckled to myself remembering what Mother and her friends would have served with this when they were entertaining in the 1950s and '60s. What came to mind immediately was tomato aspic! *So why not add it to the menu?*

Mother used to love the popovers we had at lunch at Neiman Marcus, and they seemed to be in perfect order for this little luncheon menu. You can now order the classic popover mix directly from Neiman Marcus, and I keep a supply on hand at all times.

I am very fortunate to have access to a goat cheese maker near Chestnut Cottage, so a Blueberry Goat Cheese Tart and coffee were lovely accompaniments as we exchanged memories and stories about our mothers. I love that you can easily convert this recipe into a pie if you desire.

Blueberry Goat Cheese Tarts

INGREDIENTS

For the Crust

2 cups all-purpose flour

1 stick unsalted butter, cold and cut into
    ½-inch pieces

1 tablespoon granulated sugar

Pinch of salt

Cold water (about ⅓ cup)

For the Filling

½ cup soft goat cheese

½ cup heavy cream

1 large egg

½ cup light brown sugar

¼ cup all-purpose flour

Pinch of salt

1 tablespoon fresh basil, finely chopped

4 cups fresh blueberries

For the Topping

1 cup sliced almonds

½ cup granulated sugar

⅓ cup butter, melted

For the Garnish

2 cups whipping cream, beaten to soft peaks

8 mint leaves

PREPARATION

For the Crust

Preheat oven to 350 degrees.

Combine the flour, butter, sugar, and salt in the bowl of a food processor with the chopping/mixing blade. With the processor running, let the ingredients come to a crumbly mixture with pieces about the size of a green pea. With processor still running, slowly add the cold water one tablespoon at a time until the dough forms a ball. Wrap the dough in plastic wrap and chill for about 30 minutes. Roll out the dough on a floured surface until you have room for eight 4½-inch rounds. Cut the rounds and gently press into eight muffin tins, folding over any extra dough at the top toward the outside to make a rustic crust.

For the Filling

Mix together the goat cheese, heavy cream, egg, brown sugar, flour, salt, and basil in a bowl. Add the blueberries. The texture will be like a thick batter.

For the Topping

Mix together the almonds, sugar, and butter in a bowl and set aside.

ASSEMBLING THE TARTS

Spoon the batter into the prepared tart crusts and sprinkle the topping over the top of each tart. Bake for 30 minutes until slightly bubbling and the crust is browned, rotating the tarts halfway through the baking time. Let the tarts cool at least 10 minutes on a wire rack before serving so the filling can firm up. Garnish with whipped cream and a mint leaf.

Before finishing our meal and leaving our cozy table in the courtyard for the front porch, I serve my guests yet another glass of champagne from my small antique champagne coupes. I love these little glasses because the champagne fills the stem, and you can watch the bubbles rise.

Once we're all on the front porch in the rocking chairs and the swing, we tell more fun stories about our mothers. Following our porch time, we leisurely stroll in the garden and enjoy the profusion of flowers blooming at this glorious time of spring. As a parting gift, I give each of my friends a silver picture frame for their favorite image of their mothers.

"As is the mother, so is her daughter."

—EZEKIEL 16:44

Entertaining for a Cause— Art in the Garden Tea

"There is simply the rose, it is perfect in every moment of its existence."

—RALPH WALDO EMERSON

Art in the Garden Tea Menu

A SELECTION OF TEA SANDWICHES

Egg Mayo with Watercress

Classic Cucumber

Roast Beef

Open Face Olive Pecan

BLT Stacks

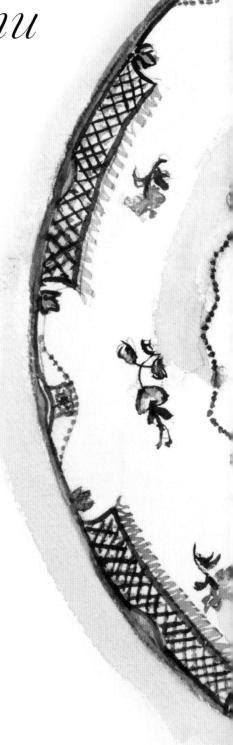

Chicken Salad in Phyllo Cups

Sausage Pinwheels

Lemon and Lavender Scones with Lemon Curd and Devonshire Cream

Petit Fours

Honey, Lavender, Vanilla, and Rose Macarons

Pecan Pie Bites

Mini Meringues with Strawberries and Lemon Curd

Loose Leaf Hot Earl Grey Tea

Iced Party Tea

Champagne

Entertaining for our favorite causes is something we often do at Chestnut Cottage. When a client who is an artist and friend said, "I have a good idea," I knew I was in trouble! I heard her "good-idea" story and immediately agreed to have a tea in our garden to raise funds for the Presbyterian Church in Waynesville. Her concept was to have local artists paint different areas of the garden. These paintings would then be on sale during the afternoon tea. The artists could sell their work for income, and the church would sell admission tickets to the event to raise funds.

On a lovely June afternoon, the tea, which we named "Art in the Garden," was attended by 100 people. It was heartwarming to see each artist's interpretation of different areas of the garden, and I enjoyed watching the guests strolling through the space. Guests were welcome to enjoy their tea in any number of places, take a closer look at the artwork, discover the garden's different features, and linger in its cozy nooks.

What could possibly be more civilized than trays filled with delectable morsels and the taste of loose-leaf tea steeped to perfection?

As soon as the artists started putting up their work, I knew I simply couldn't resist the painting of our foxgloves by local artist Jenny Buckner. It now hangs in our master bedroom.

Other wonderful artists at the tea were Margaret Roberts, who painted the colorful likeness of our window boxes; Jo Ridge Kelly, whose delphinium painting was a somewhat abstract interpretation of those in the garden; and Bee Sieburg, who painted our upper terrace and a sweet little painting of hollyhocks.

Bee also generously painted a lovely lily that we reproduced on a bookmark and gave to each attendee as a memento of the tea. If you visit the interior of Chestnut Cottage, you'll find several of Bee's paintings that Wells and I commissioned. We are definitely big fans of her work! Margaret painted the lovely watercolor of the back door of Chestnut Cottage,

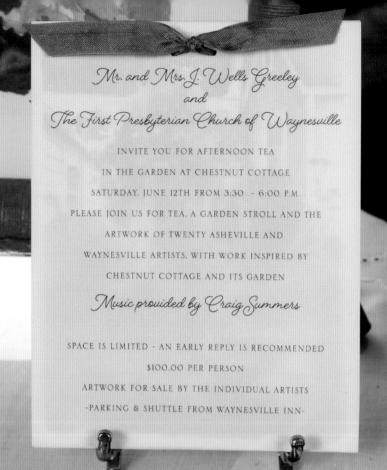

Mr. and Mrs. J. Wells Greeley
and
The First Presbyterian Church of Waynesville

INVITE YOU FOR AFTERNOON TEA
IN THE GARDEN AT CHESTNUT COTTAGE
SATURDAY, JUNE 12TH FROM 3:30 - 6:00 P.M.
PLEASE JOIN US FOR TEA, A GARDEN STROLL AND THE
ARTWORK OF TWENTY ASHEVILLE AND
WAYNESVILLE ARTISTS, WITH WORK INSPIRED BY
CHESTNUT COTTAGE AND ITS GARDEN

Music provided by Craig Summers

SPACE IS LIMITED - AN EARLY REPLY IS RECOMMENDED
$100.00 PER PERSON

ARTWORK FOR SALE BY THE INDIVIDUAL ARTISTS
-PARKING & SHUTTLE FROM WAYNESVILLE INN-

which was used on the invitation for the tea. She kindly gave me that beautiful painting as a gift when I finished the design work on her home.

I love the antique French easel that artist Jo Ridge Kelly used for her beautiful delphinium painting.

Duncan MacDuff likes to sun himself on our upper terrace and mistakenly thought he was invited to have a plate of tea sandwiches and a nice glass of champagne!

When I first realized I would be hosting 100 people, I immediately went to work on all the components that make an afternoon tea so special. I am a big fan of this special occasion and have long enjoyed it both stateside and abroad. What could possibly be more civilized than trays filled with delectable morsels and the taste of loose-leaf tea steeped to perfection?

Table Inspiration

But even more than the food, I love the elements of the tea table: lush flower arrangements, a collection of different patterns of china, and gleaming silver. Of course, I always start with the color concept. Blue and white is in no short supply at Chestnut Cottage, and I believe it to be the most classic of all color schemes.

One of the favorite aspects of my design career has been the array of beautiful fabrics I have been privileged to use. The foundation of my tea table vision was a delightful blue and white tree of life print ("Bagatelle" from Manuel Canovas in Bleu De Chine) on linen in bold colors, built up from a series of intricate patterns. This tablecloth pattern definitely called for blue and white containers for floral arrangements and in the china patterns I would select.

Many years ago, while shopping at Replacements, I found two stacks of Nikko's "Victoria Blue" accent plates on sale. They were a very good price, so I bought fifty. I thought with all of the blue and white at Chestnut Cottage, they would be perfect for larger cocktail parties or teas. I soon discovered that collecting different blue and white patterns in teacups would also be an asset for afternoon teas.

Since Art in the Garden was an outdoor gathering, I wanted to have plenty of fresh-cut florals on the tables. So blue and white vases and vessels came out from cabinets, down from the tops of armoires, and up from storage in the tiny basement at Chestnut Cottage. Old and new blue and white always seem to live together harmoniously.

"It's always tea-time!"

—THE MAD HATTER,
ALICE'S ADVENTURES IN WONDERLAND

At this particular gathering, tall blue and white vases held lush arrangements of bells of Ireland, delphiniums, hydrangeas, Queen Anne's lace, white lisianthus, and a variety of ferns.

As guests entered the lower walled garden, they were greeted with oversized blue and white bowls filled with white geraniums and ivy. This elegant yet understated pairing of blue and white vessels with green and white cuttings allowed the colorful art—and the garden itself—to truly stand out.

This garden tea was also a perfect opportunity for me to use my collection of silver pieces. Our tea service was a wedding gift from two dear friends, and I was able to find tiny sugar cubes with blue and white flowers to fill the sugar bowl. I added antique tea strainers and sugar tongs to the tea tray as a finishing touch. When I visit antique shops anywhere in the world, I'm always keeping an eye out for special items such as these to include in an afternoon tea. As I will say many times in this book, collections are made to be used and enjoyed!

As I will say many times in this book, collections are made to be used and enjoyed!

Trays filled with a selection of classic tea sandwiches, lemon and lavender scones, petit fours, and honey, vanilla, lavender, and rose macarons were set out for guests to enjoy as they strolled the garden. We also served chicken salad made with my homemade lime pickles set in phyllo cups and individual meringues filled with lemon curd and strawberries. Who doesn't love a warm scone with lemon curd and Devonshire cream and a nice cup of hot tea?

The last—but certainly not the least—menu item was my prized Sausage Pinwheels. I enjoy making these for tea parties, but also for cocktail events. This savory treat paired well with the sweet offerings of this menu and the variety of tea sandwiches. These pinwheels take a bit of time to make, but they are well worth the effort.

Afternoon Tea in the Garden Menu

A SELECTION OF TEA SANDWICHES
EGG MAYO WITH WATERCRESS
CLASSIC CUCUMBER
ROAST BEEF
OPEN FACE OLIVE PECAN
BLT STACKS

CHICKEN SALAD IN PHYLLO CUPS

SAUSAGE PINWHEELS

LEMON AND LAVENDAR SCONES WITH LEMON CURD
AND DEVONSHIRE CREAM

PETIT FOURS

HONEY LAVENDAR, VANILLA AND ROSE MACARONS

PECAN PIE BITES

MINI MERINGUES WITH STRAWBERRIES AND LEMON CURD

LOOSE LEAF HOT EARL GREY TEA
ICED PARTY TEA
CHAMPAGNE

Sausage Pinwheels

INGREDIENTS

8 ounces ground Italian sausage

½ 17.3-ounce package of frozen puff pastry, which is 1 sheet

½ cup shredded Fontina cheese

¼ cup roasted red peppers, chopped

2 tablespoons fresh basil, chopped

2 tablespoons freshly grated Parmesan cheese

¼ teaspoon garlic salt

¼ teaspoon dried Italian herbs

⅛ teaspoon ground black pepper

1 large egg

1 tablespoon water

Note: You can use 4 ounces of mild Italian sausage and 4 ounces of hot Italian sausage for a spicier pinwheel.

PREPARATION

Preheat oven to 400 degrees.

In a skillet, cook sausage over medium heat until no longer pink, stirring occasionally to break into crumbles. Drain sausage on paper towels and let cool completely.

Place a sheet of parchment paper on a baking sheet. Let the puff pastry thaw just enough to be able to roll up and encase the sausage mixture filling. It should still be cold and firm. On a lightly floured surface, unroll puff pastry sheet. Using a rolling pin, roll out sheet to a 12x10-inch rectangle.

Scatter cooked sausage over the puff pastry, leaving a 1-inch empty border around the edges. Scatter Fontina cheese, roasted peppers, basil, Parmesan cheese, garlic salt, Italian herbs, and black pepper over the sausage. Starting at a long edge, roll up pastry firmly and evenly to encase ingredients and form a cylinder.

Use dampened fingers to pinch seam closed and rotate the seam to the underside of the cylinder. Tuck ends under. Place in the freezer for 30 minutes.

Using a serrated bread knife and a gentle sawing motion, cut 15 ½-inch slices from the cylinder. Place slices 2 inches apart on the prepared baking sheet. In a small bowl, whisk together egg and 1 tablespoon of water. Brush the tops and sides of the slices with the egg mixture.

Bake for 13–15 minutes or until golden brown. Serve immediately.

Note: You may freeze cylinders wrapped in plastic wrap and placed in freezer bags to use as needed later. The cylinders should not be completely thawed before cutting.

I believe the pleasures of afternoon tea stay long in our memories. When I was a young child at my grandmother's house, she served all the grandchildren hot tea with sugar and milk. We eagerly awaited our "cream tea" in the afternoons. My maternal grandfather was from Northern Ireland, so once again, our drink of choice was pretty much a given, and it was always hot tea. I drink hot tea year-round and always with milk or cream. One must not depart from their raising! Fluffy scones with lemon curd and clotted cream and tiny cucumber sandwiches, along with Earl Grey tea, evoke many of my happy childhood memories. When I recall having tea in London at The Ritz, Claridge's, and Fortnum & Mason, it makes me yearn to repeat this elegant ritual.

There's a lot to be said for treating yourself as elegantly as you do your guests!

Among tea drinkers, the debate continues over the ubiquitous tea bag. For many years, the tea in tea bags was of a lesser quality than that of loose tea. In recent years, however, many good tea companies such as Twinings and Fortnum & Mason have vastly improved the reputation of the tea bag by packing better quality tea and in a greater variety. High-quality Earl Grey, Darjeeling, and English and Irish Breakfast now come in tea bags. I will confess that I sometimes use teas bags when I am in the middle of a hectic day. They are just convenient! However, the loose version simply makes a better cup of tea. Part of the joy of afternoon tea is the ritual, and crustless tea sandwiches, scones, and loose tea are part of that ritual for me. Even when you are not entertaining others, the ritual of teatime can be a relaxing and civilized break from a busy day.

"... there are few hours in life more agreeable than the hour dedicated to the ceremony known as afternoon tea."

—HENRY JAMES,
PORTRAIT OF A LADY

Since not everyone likes hot tea, I decided to offer champagne at Art in the Garden, along with my own special recipe, Iced Party Tea. This Iced Party Tea is a refreshing blend of tea, lemonade, and ginger ale, and I have made this beverage for years. It is easy to make and very popular with tea drinkers and non-tea drinkers alike.

When the sun began to set and all the guests had gone, we relaxed in the garden with a glass of champagne and were so delighted that several artists were able to sell their work and the church made a nice income from the sale of the tickets. Being a part of any community should lead us to help those causes about which we are passionate. And just remember: Entertaining for a cause allows you to use your own unique creativity in ways that might surprise you!

Iced Party Tea

INGREDIENTS

3 quarts medium-strength black tea

½ cup sugar

1 12-ounce can frozen lemonade
   concentrate

1 quart ginger ale, cold

10 lemon slices

Mint leaves for garnish

PREPARATION

Steep 2 family-sized black tea bags in 3 quarts
of hot water. Dissolve sugar in the tea while it is
still warm and add in the lemonade concentrate.
Chill thoroughly. Just before serving, stir in the
cold ginger ale. Serve over crushed ice and garnish with a slice of lemon and mint leaves.

Yields 10 8-ounce servings.

Collecting

Silver, Crystal Boxes, and Tommy Mitchell Botanicals

Entertaining at Chestnut Cottage often involves my silver collection, and Easter is no exception. For many, many years I have collected both sterling pieces and plate silver. I keep my silver serving pieces in an English armoire in the master bedroom. That may seem a bit odd, but storage at Chestnut Cottage is a challenge, and I love opening up the armoire and seeing all the silver serving pieces in one place. Recently I had my faux finisher, Anna Krause, wash the inside of the armoire in a lovely blue color that I pulled from the drapery and upholstery fabrics in the bedroom. This color really complements the silver, and it's just a happy hue for me. I would be remiss not to share a few of my favorite pieces in the collection and tell you a bit about them.

Perhaps my very favorite and also the most intriguing pieces are two "dish rings," often called Irish potato rings. A dinner table or sideboard silver accessory in the form of a hollow cylinder or spool-shaped ring, they were introduced at the end of the seventeenth century in England and Ireland. They support food dishes on the dining table and protect the wood surface from the heat of hot food. Some dish rings are the same diameter at the top and bottom rims, but most have different widths on the rim so they can be reversed to support containers of different sizes. From the 1740s forward, dish rings were usually spool shaped, and their incurved sides provided silversmiths a place to create elaborate decorative patterns using techniques that included piercing, chasing, and engraving. One of my rings is marked "S.H. Waterhouse," which is an Irish (Dublin) mark, and the other has a Scottish (Edinburgh) mark. Both depict rural village and forest scenes.

Two silver baskets that I most often use as Duncan's and Wells's Easter baskets are also perfect for bread. Both are English plate, one with a fern detailing and a shell center, and the other with a scalloped form pierced foliate border with a gadrooned shaped edge. These baskets also make a nice container for flowers if you use a vintage frog.

My English Victorian condiment holder was given to me by Wells's mother and is late nineteenth century. The set includes three cut crystal cruets with stoppers, two bottles with perforated caps for salt and pepper, and a mustard or jelly jar with a hinged and notched lid to hold a small spoon. These sets can look lovely on today's tables for the very same purposes. The cruets, used for vinegars or oils, would be perfect for a nice olive oil paired with a balsamic vinegar and a champagne vinegar.

One of the most unusual pieces in my silver collection is a cheese-ball holder. I hardly believed the antique dealer when he told me what it was. However, I was intrigued, and I couldn't resist it, mainly for its novelty. After a bit of research, I determined that indeed it was an English Victorian cheese-ball holder for Edam or Gouda cheese. It would hardly work for any of the soft cheese or chicken balls that I make, but I keep it in my collection because it amuses me. The cheese ball is placed on the holder, and a screw is turned to tighten the arms to hold the cheese firmly in place for displaying and serving. I have tried it with Edam, and it does work. Dining became an art form during the Victorian Age and, as this cheese-ball holder confirms, the Victorians had a silver serving piece for everything imaginable.

A petit four server was another unusual item Victorian women added to their collections. My set of beautiful sterling silver petit four/mignardise cutlery is French (Paris). The ornate handles are made of sterling silver, and the top has a gilt wash. Mine was a gift, and it came in its original green leather case. Mignardises are elegant, bite-size pastries and other desserts that are traditionally served at the end of a meal, and this four-piece set contains different pieces for serving a variety of treats. One can use this set for a truly sophisticated end to a meal or for tea. I use mine at afternoon tea.

The silver vase that gets used constantly at Chestnut Cottage is an American sterling piece from Boston's Maynard and Potter, Inc. It has a formed basket (that is footed, tapered, and pierced with a horizontal ring binding) and a glass vase insert.

The fun part of a silver collection is that most pieces can be used for a variety of purposes. About twice a year, we have a silver cleaning day, and I enjoy seeing all the small details on the individual pieces come alive.

As I sit surrounded by all of the flowers in the garden, my Tommy Mitchell botanical collection easily comes to mind. For many years, I have been a fan of this incredible artist. Tommy's career began as an art restorer. He was particularly intrigued with metal sculpture and began creating his own floral pieces. In talking to Tommy, he tells me his inspiration comes from both his travels and from antique botanical studies.

He works in a combination of copper, brass, and steel pieces covered in paint and gold leaf. Each piece is handmade and signed. I have placed his work on my design projects, and I have my own pieces here at Chestnut Cottage. For my personal collection, I asked Tommy to create flowers that were actually growing in our garden. My collection of his work lives in the master bedroom, where at the end of a long day, I can have flowers all around me no matter what season of the year it is.

No Easter would be complete without an Easter basket for Wells and Duncan. On occasion, they get their treats in two of my prized silver baskets.

As a gift for his sixtieth birthday, I gave Wells this lovely English sterling loving cup. The cup has three family shields, representing the union of three families. This piece is late nineteenth century with a Martin, Hall and Co. mark. As you can see, it is perfect for chilling a bottle of champagne or wine.

An English Sheffield biscuit box is a luxurious way to serve cookies or scones. The bun feet, the ringed lion handles, and a small bone handle are interesting details. The top has a shallow engraved stylized foliate decoration.

The domed egg warmer is English with the Mappin and Webb mark and has a bone handle as well as a locking mechanism. I can't imagine why one would want to lock the eggs, or any other breakfast item for that matter! It does, however, add a lovely touch to the breakfast table.

I found this fun butter keeper on an antiquing trip to Ireland many years ago. This piece is English, circa 1853. It is marked "Cartright and Hirons" and has a pierced top, crowned with a standing cow. Inside is a white glass insert to drain your butter.

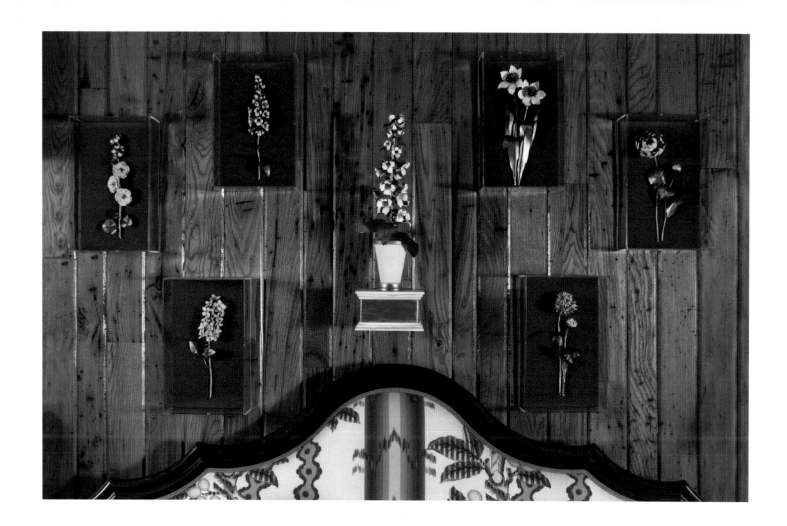

After initially struggling to decide whether the flowers should be white and gold or painted in their actual hues, I opted for the simpler of the two. I feel the white and gold treatment brings a peaceful, but crisp element to the design of the bedroom.

The grouping over my bed includes a peony, bee balm, a daffodil, a foxglove, a lilac, a delphinium, and a hollyhock—all in this style that is so emblematic of Tommy's iconic work.

Because he has so many design options for his botanicals, I also chose flowers in acrylic boxes for the wall, as well as some in small gold and white containers to place on brackets and tabletops. For the containers, I selected a tulip, an orchid, a lily of the valley, a lilac, and a primrose. Each time I visit Tommy at market, I see new works of art that I think I can't possibly live without. However, I've run out of wall space at the cottage!

Small collections like these that bring us joy should always be included in the overall design of every room.

Small collections like these that bring us joy should always be included in the overall design of every room.

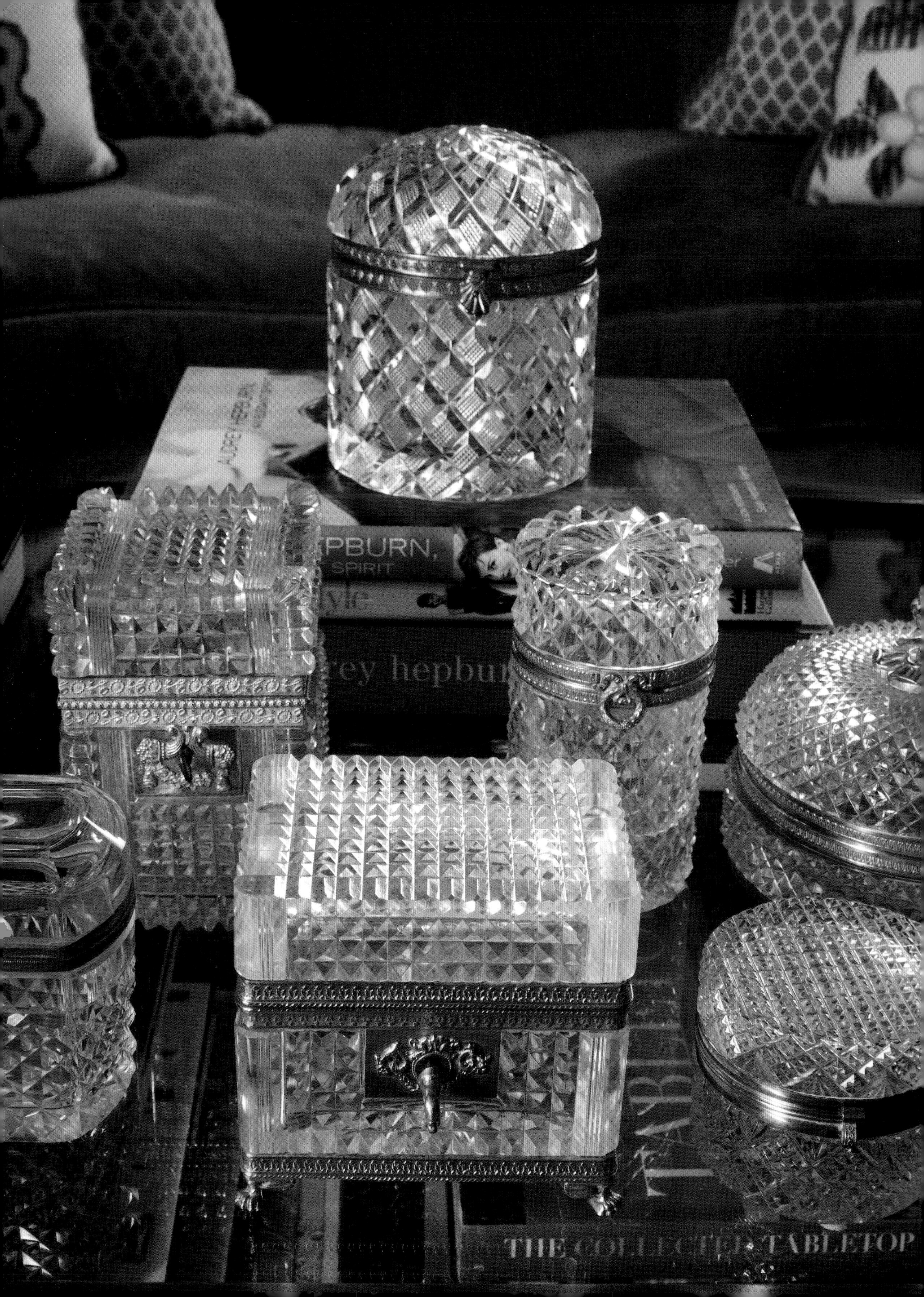
EPBURN,
SPIRIT
rey hepbur
THE COLLECTE TABLETOP

Tommy's botanicals mix nicely with another collection in our master bedroom of French Baccarat crystal boxes. I first became fascinated with these while on a trip to France. In Beaune, around the corner from a winery, I found two in a tiny antique shop and another collection was born.

These boxes come in a variety of shapes, and mine are generally from the nineteenth century. Most are diamond cut and are often called casket boxes or dresser boxes. Most of mine have bronze and ormolu details and are stylized versions of earlier, more functional boxes that were used to securely store valuables such as jewelry.

It would be hard to choose a favorite among these French boxes, as I am intrigued by each one's intricate detailing. The large, round, domed piece has a shell motif in the ormolu. The heavily cut square box has a floral motif in the ormolu mount with a floral garland around the lock and key. Another round piece is topped with a bronze acorn and has tiny round bronze feet. One of the rectangular domed pieces also has a floral garland encircling the lock, with very detailed claw feet. A thin rectangular box has an uncut top. How could anyone pick a favorite from this group? Much like the Tommy Mitchell botanicals, this collection's raison d'être is the great joy its beauty brings!

Simple Pleasures

ASPARAGUS TART

One of my simple pleasures of spring is fresh asparagus! As I grow no vegetables in the Chestnut Cottage garden, I always get my fresh spring asparagus at the farmer's market. This asparagus is grown locally and is always so fresh and tasty. You may have noticed my Chilled Asparagus in Walnut Vinaigrette on the Easter Menu. As long as the asparagus continues to come in, I love making this Asparagus, Goat Cheese, and Tarragon Tart. Goat cheese from the local Dark Cove Farms makes this recipe so very creamy, and the fresh tarragon from my herb garden adds to the lovely taste. You don't have to make your own crust, so it's an easy, quick recipe. I recommend that you serve this tart warm within an hour of baking so it will be at its absolute best. The crisp pastry shatters into buttery bits when you bite down on the still runny cheese! It makes a nice appetizer cut into squares, but I usually serve it with a simple salad for lunch or as a side for dinner.

Asparagus, Goat Cheese, and Tarragon Tart

INGREDIENTS

1 cup soft goat cheese, at room
temperature

1 large egg, lightly beaten, at room
temperature

1 clove garlic, minced

1½ tablespoons fresh tarragon leaves,
chopped

½ tablespoon lemon zest

½ teaspoon fine sea salt (plus more
for sprinkling on top after baking,
if desired)

Pinch of freshly grated nutmeg

All-purpose flour, for dusting the
work surface for the pastry

1 cup crème fraîche, at room
temperature

1 sheet of all-butter puff pastry,
thawed if previously frozen

8 ounces thin asparagus, woody
ends removed

Extra-virgin olive oil

2 tablespoons grated Parmesan cheese

½ teaspoon freshly ground black pepper

¼ teaspoon red pepper flakes

½ cup of shaved Parmesan cheese

PREPARATION

Preheat oven to 425 degrees. In a medium bowl, use a fork to mash together the goat cheese, egg, garlic, tarragon, lemon zest, salt, and nutmeg until smooth. Using a hand mixer, beat in the créme fraîche until smooth.

On a lightly floured surface, roll out puff pastry into a 13x11-inch rectangle about ⅛ inch thick. Transfer the dough to a parchment-lined cookie sheet. With a sharp knife, lightly score a ½-inch border around the edges of the puff pastry. Spread the crème fraîche mixture evenly inside the scored border. Line up the asparagus spears on top and brush them with olive oil. Sprinkle some sea salt according to taste, along with the grated Parmesan cheese.

Bake until the pastry is puffed and golden, about 25–30 minutes. As soon as you take the tart out of the oven, sprinkle with black pepper, red pepper flakes, and the shaved Parmesan. Let set for about 8–10 minutes before serving. Drizzle a little olive oil on top when serving.

As late spring comes to an end, it is time to savor the joys of summer: There will be more outdoor entertaining for another favorite cause, indoor entertaining events, new surprises in the garden, more collections from around the cottage, and recipes to inspire your entertaining. So come along for summer at Chestnut Cottage!

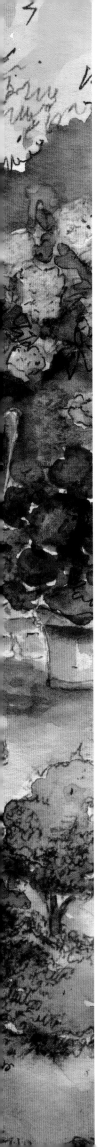

Summer

"*Then followed that beautiful season . . . summer . . .*
Filled was the air with a dreamy and
magical light; and the landscape
Lay as if new created in all the freshness of childhood."

—HENRY WADSWORTH LONGFELLOW

My Garden

A garden is a quiet, lovely place
Wherein to walk alone in thoughtful mood;
Where, though you see not every flower's face,
Each gives a sweetness that will fill the air
With loveliness supreme; with peace that claims
Your inmost being as you wander there.
Let traffic speed and trundle up the hill—
You hear it not—because the soul is still.

—HILDA G. GARNER
FROM *MY GARDEN*

In the Garden

The summer garden at Chestnut Cottage brings new surprises each day. I can safely say that we do indeed have a collection of hydrangeas. A large area in the back garden is filled with 'Oak Leaf' hydrangeas, and we have several in the front garden as well. You'll find 'Limelight,' 'Little Limes,' 'Annabelle,' 'Lacecap,' 'Endless Summer,' and 'Nikko Blue' dotted throughout both spaces.

Yet my favorite is the Hydrangea paniculata 'Unique.' It's the only type of hydrangea that can become a tree, and we have two that have manifested in that form. They were at Chestnut Cottage when I first purchased the property. They appear to be one tree but are actually two that have become so entwined that they've grown together and formed a high canopy. Not only do they anchor the front garden, but they bring me great joy each year.

As summer progresses, the 'Little Limes' turn a lovely shade of pink and the 'Limelights' a soft green.

The bee balm is beginning to put on a beautiful red show and makes such an interesting contrast against the white 'Oak Leaf' hydrangeas.

Dahlias are starting to come up in the garden, and the coneflowers and the astilbe are in bloom.

Iridescent-blue thistle seems to keep its head turned toward the summer sun.

The butter-yellow hollyhocks are towering above the border, and the window boxes and containers pour forth in a profusion of color.

Most of our window boxes and containers get sun. However, a few are what I refer to as our "shade containers." When you drive up to Chestnut Cottage and stop in our upper car park, you are greeted with a pair of three-tiered containers filled with cheerful 'Scarlet Red' begonias, white 'New Guinea' impatiens, 'Kimberly Queen' ferns, ivy, and the lovely little 'Gingerland' caladiums.

Summer chores in the garden are not as time consuming as they were in spring. But you have to remember to keep the garden well watered and the plants deadheaded. During this season, you must also remember to take the time to order next year's bulbs, so your favorites aren't sold out! And, of course, don't forget to give all the topiaries another little haircut.

We are trying to get dahlias established in the garden, but we've faced challenges. Because the soil is very compacted clay and we receive lots of rain, we decided the dahlias needed to first be planted in nursery pots and then put in the ground to keep them from rotting in the wet clay soil. In an effort to keep pesky bunnies away and to prevent tall plants from bending over, we caged the dahlias this year. And, to my delight, they are beginning to be stars in the summer garden here at Chestnut Cottage.

I plan to lift the tubers from the nursery pots at the end of the season and save them for next year. My main reason for growing dahlias is to be able to cut them for floral

arrangements—so perhaps they *will be* worth the trouble! During the summer, our border plantings seem to change daily. I love the overflowing daisies alongside Nicotiana, the black and blue salvia, and the jewelweed, which is also known as touch-me-not.

The phlox are brilliant in the borders and are also good for cutting. This time of year, the herb garden outside the kitchen is full of fresh basil, parsley, thyme, rosemary, sage, lemon verbena, and lots of mint. The herbs stand at the ready for summer meals and entertaining.

As the season progresses, the garden gradually starts to wind down and begin its transition into autumn.

"For the love of gardening is a seed that once sown never dies, but always grows and grows to an enduring and ever-lasting source of happiness."

—GERTRUDE JEKYLL

Gatherings

Entertaining for a Cause— Top Dog!

Top Dog! Menu

Cheese Board with Rosemary Parmesan "Westie" Crackers

Gourmet Hot Dog Selection

Cheesy Mexican Hot Dogs

Greek Hot Dogs

Bacon Wrapped Jalapeño Hot Dogs

French Onion Hot Dogs

Onion Rings

Peach, Blueberry, and Blackberry Cobbler with Ice Cream

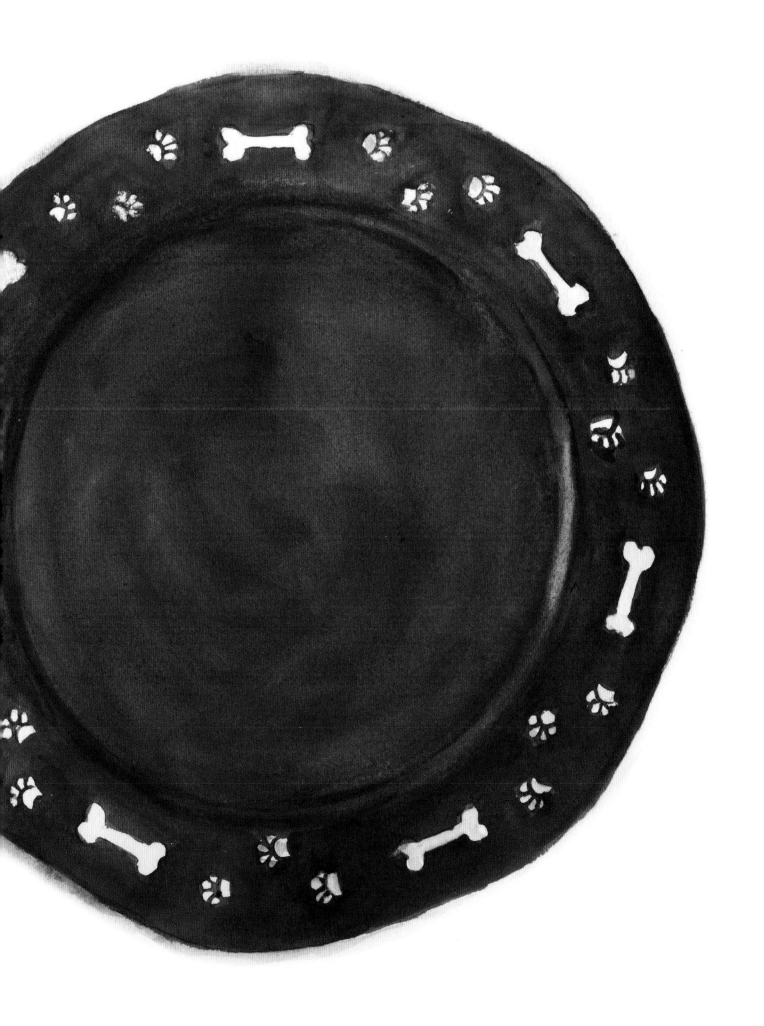

Summer continues to bring more outdoor entertaining opportunities to Chestnut Cottage. Although we spend a great deal of our summers at our lakeside retreat, Chatuge Cottage, we try to plan fun gatherings at Chestnut Cottage during this season as well. Our hearts were warmed by the money raised for a local church and local artists at the Art in the Garden Tea. But there's another cause that is even nearer and dearer to our hearts.

Many years ago, we fell in love with a breed of dogs that can only be described as independent, highly intelligent, clever, alert, curious, playful, and full of self-esteem. I'm talking about the White West Highland Terrier, commonly known as the Westie.

Our first Westie, Bentley Greeley, lived a long, happy, and spoiled life of eighteen years at Chestnut Cottage. Bentley was a perfect dog in most all ways. He was very intelligent and alert, he was indeed independent, and he could even be described as arrogant! At the very least, you could say he had no shortage of self-esteem. After his death, we buried our sweet boy in the garden at Chestnut Cottage beside his boxwood topiary. We grieved for him for three years, and I knew in my heart there would never be a Westie as perfect as our Bentley.

Then one day, while I was giving a talk about *The Collected Tabletop* at the Cathedral Antique Show in Atlanta, I emotionally mentioned Bentley and how very much we missed him. As I was signing books later, a lovely woman in line slipped me a piece of paper naming a "wonderful Westie breeder in Atlanta." Her knowing smile told me she knew the breeder well. I tucked the note into my purse and once back at home, I put it away in my bedside table. That little note called out to me daily. One Sunday afternoon in late November, I called Mardot Kennels in Atlanta. The delightful breeder, Marleen Burford, assured me that her Westies were outstanding, and she would be happy to put me on her list for a male puppy. A few months later, Marleen rang and said she had a puppy for us. The picture she sent sealed the deal. It was love at first sight! A month later, Duncan MacDuff joined us at Chestnut Cottage.

I'm an only child and have never had children, but I have heard that children in a family often have very different personalities. Like Bentley, Duncan is independent, clever, curious, and has plenty of self-esteem. But he has a lot of characteristics that are all his own: He is mischievous, extremely loving, and friendly—and not in the least bit arrogant! To say that we are in love with this breed would be an understatement.

While I have to admit I have somewhat of a love-hate relationship with social media, one joy it consistently brings me are all my newfound Westie friends from around the world.

Please Join Wells and Kathy Greeley
For Cocktails and Dinner
To Celebrate Westie Rescue

Saturday July 24th, 2021 at 6:00 pm
280 Rolling Drive
Please Respond To
kathryn@kathryngreeleydesigns.com

There's Ralphy; Hammish and Jazz; BBgirlldog in Australia; Luna in Switzerland; Haku in Japan; Olliex in South Korea; Kapu in Finland; Celine in Venezuela; Nala and Nisha in Germany—as well as Parker and Duncan and many other stateside Westie friends.

But Duncan MacDuff's special friend is sweet Winnie, who lives in California. It was through Winnie's parents, Anne and Massimo Guerrini, that I learned about WROC, Westie Rescue of Orange County and Beyond. Their mission is to rescue, rehabilitate, and place Westies in permanent homes. Their primary focus is securing loving homes for unwanted, neglected, or abused animals. In addition, they provide the public with education about the needs of this special breed. This organization is truly volunteer based, with no paid positions. Furthermore, the organization works hard for *all* their dogs, regardless of health issues, age, or behavior.

Whether you are endeared to Westies or not, WROC has the ability to both put a smile on your face and bring a tear to your eye with the love they have for these dogs. It was heartbreaking to see the condition of some of the Westies they rescued. But once in the care of WROC, these dogs blossom and can be placed in loving forever homes. When I started following Kay Deloach and Jill Sater, who are both affiliated with the organization, I was so very touched by their dedicated work and what they are doing for Westies. I can't tell you the kick I get from seeing groups of smiling Westies dressed up for every holiday. The most amazing sights are the Westies that have learned to surf! Kay's Petey appears to be quite the champion. You can just see that Westie determination on Petey's face when he roars ashore.

Inspired by these friends, their stories, and my abounding love for Westies, I decided to host a Westie Rescue Benefit dinner at Chestnut Cottage. So out came our doggie table-cloth and moss dog topiaries—and a dinner party was born.

Duncan MacDuff insisted that this be a classy event for his worldwide friends, so it started with a black and white Westie invitation.

This clever dog even asked for a private label wine for his party. Sadly, his social media friends from around the world couldn't make it to Chestnut Cottage, but he found friends and Westie lovers closer to home who were happy to support his cause. And since we were familiar with the California winery Mutt Lynch from a previous event, Duncan ordered chardonnay, rosé, and cabernet sauvignon on his own private label—"Leader of the Pack"—for the event.

It was a lovely summer evening on the sunken front lawn at Chestnut Cottage, with the 'Rose of Sharon' (*Hibiscus syriacus*), several varieties of hydrangeas, and the yellow 'Teasing Georgia' roses all in bloom.

And, of course, Duncan MacDuff was dressed in his best black tie to host the event.

Table Inspiration

In truth, Duncan is a great lover of all dogs—not just Westies. So a tablecloth depicting several breeds was the natural starting point for my table design, and chairs donned "houndstooth" fabric covers. Topiaries of a Westie, a poodle, and a golden retriever were watching over the table from above.

For the dinnerware, I selected the "Cantaria" pattern from Skyros Designs, a line I often sell in my design practice. Two colors alternate in the pattern—persimmon and golden honey. These hues coordinated perfectly with the palette of the tablecloth. "Cantaria" means *stonework* in Portuguese, and aptly describes this beautifully created dinnerware line. Handcrafted in Portugal of ceramic stoneware, this pattern can go from the freezer to the oven to the dishwasher! Through the years, I have also found it to be very chip resistant. And finally, I love its organic shape and hammered texture that offers a traditional look combined with modern elegance.

Both colors of the dinnerware were set on black leather chargers and framed with twig cutlery and tortoise stemware.

Napkins (solid black and dog-bone motifs) were held securely in place with tiny black dog collars that doubled as napkin rings.

I chose shades of orange and green flowers that offered lots of texture, crowned by the three moss, dog-shaped topiaries.

As I truly believe that Westies are "the top" (dog), I tucked the lyrics to "You're the Top" by Cole Porter into the menu-card holder.

We started the evening with glasses of wine from Leader of the Pack. An antique French breadboard was ladened with a variety of cheese offerings, olives, and our home-made Rosemary-Parmesan Westie Crackers.

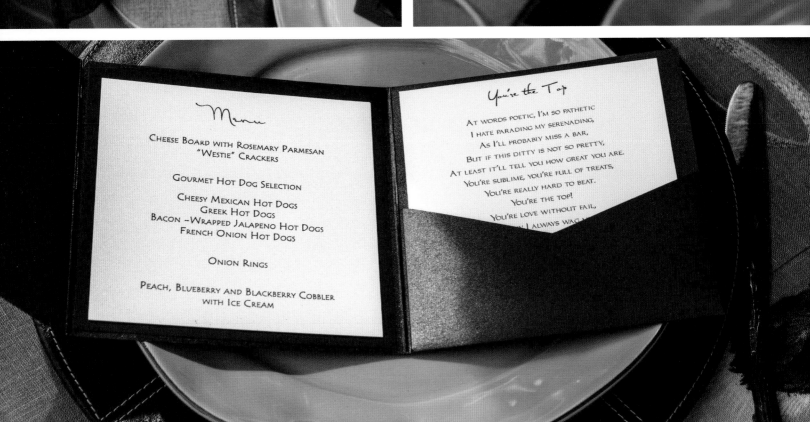

Menu

CHEESE BOARD WITH ROSEMARY PARMESAN
"WESTIE" CRACKERS

GOURMET HOT DOG SELECTION
CHEESY MEXICAN HOT DOGS
GREEK HOT DOGS
BACON-WRAPPED JALAPENO HOT DOGS
FRENCH ONION HOT DOGS

ONION RINGS

PEACH, BLUEBERRY AND BLACKBERRY COBBLER
WITH ICE CREAM

You're the Top

AT WORDS POETIC, I'M SO PATHETIC
I HATE PARADING MY SERENADING,
AS I'LL PROBABLY MISS A BAR,
BUT IF THIS DITTY IS NOT SO PRETTY,
AT LEAST IT'LL TELL YOU HOW GREAT YOU ARE.
YOU'RE SUBLIME, YOU'RE FULL OF TREATS,
YOU'RE REALLY HARD TO BEAT.
YOU'RE THE TOP!
YOU'RE LOVE WITHOUT FAIL,
I ALWAYS WAG

Rosemary-Parmesan Westie Crackers

INGREDIENTS

¾ cup all-purpose flour

1 teaspoon salt

1 teaspoon coarsely ground pepper

1 teaspoon fresh rosemary needles, chopped
(do not use the stems)

4 tablespoons (½ stick) chilled unsalted
butter, cut into ½-inch pieces

1 cup grated Parmigiano-Reggiano cheese

¼ cup heavy cream, chilled

PREPARATION

In the bowl of a food processor, combine flour, salt, pepper, and rosemary and pulse twice to mix. Add the butter and pulse until the mixture resembles coarse meal, about 10 pulses. Add the cheese and pulse twice to combine. With the processor motor running, pour in the cream and continue processing until the dough forms a single mass. Wrap the dough in plastic wrap and refrigerate for about 1 hour.

Preheat oven to 325 degrees. Line a baking sheet with parchment paper. Remove dough from the refrigerator, place on a floured surface, and roll out to about ⅛ inch thick. Cut out the dough with a Westie cookie cutter and evenly place Westies on the parchment-lined baking sheet. Bake on convection setting until the crackers are golden brown, approximately 20–25 minutes.

Remove baking sheet from oven and place on a wire rack. When the crackers are cool to the touch, remove from the sheet and transfer to the rack to finish cooling. This recipe makes between 20–24 crackers, depending on the shape and size of the cutter. Store in an airtight container at room temperature.

Note: Of course, you can cut the dough into any shape or roll it into a log and cut in rounds. But for this dinner, a Westie cutter was a must!

For the main course at this event, what could possibly be more appropriate than hot dogs? The menu featured a selection of gourmet, globally inspired hot dogs, including cheesy Mexican, Greek, bacon-wrapped jalapeño, and French onion hot dogs, served with crispy onion rings.

At Chestnut Cottage, informal summer entertaining always calls for a good cobbler as dessert. And our local farmer's market happened to be offering beautiful peaches, blueberries, and blackberries. Since I was unable to decide on just one fruit for the cobbler, I finally decided to mix the three!

Over the years, I have learned that making cobbler in a big black cast-iron skillet gives it the perfect amount of chewy crust. I am loyal to the "dump-it-in" method, and the cobblers always come out moist and chewy. Topped with vanilla ice cream, cobblers are indeed a summer delight.

Dump-It-In Fruit Cobbler

INGREDIENTS

1½ cups self-rising flour

1½ cups granulated sugar

1½ cups whole milk

1½ sticks unsalted butter, chilled

1 cup ripe, fresh peaches, peeled
    and sliced

1 cup ripe, fresh blackberries

1 cup ripe, fresh blueberries

PREPARATION

Preheat oven to 350 degrees. Place butter in a 9x13-inch baking dish or a 13-inch cast-iron frying pan, and place in the oven just long enough to melt the butter. Then remove and set aside. I think the cast-iron pan makes for a nicer crust.

Mix together the flour, sugar, and milk. Pour this mixture on top of the melted butter. Carefully spread the fruit over the top of the flour mixture. Do not mix!

Bake for 30–40 minutes until the crust turns golden brown.

Serve the warm cobbler with vanilla ice cream.

"Summer afternoon, summer afternoon; to me those have always been the two most beautiful words in the English language."

—HENRY JAMES,
AN INTERNATIONAL EPISODE

Each guest was asked to consider making a donation for a better life for rescued Westies. Duncan rewarded each donor with a bottle of his Leader of the Pack wine as a remembrance of the evening.

It's just hard to beat a summer evening in the yard for relaxing dinners!

Shades of Blue Birthday

I love to spend summer afternoons in the company of friends. What better way to do just that than by celebrating a good friend's birthday? I am a big fan of going all out for birthdays and think that we always feel special when somebody gives a birthday party in our honor.

One of my best friends Holli Morris shares with me a deep love for blue and white collecting. You might remember Holli's home from my first book, *The Collected Tabletop*! Since we both collect blue and white, I thought a Shades of Blue luncheon would be a perfect way to celebrate her birthday.

Table Inspiration

The kitchen table seemed to be a good venue for our party, as we would be surrounded by the blue and white that are a part of my everyday decor. With a range of orange dahlias blooming in the garden, I was inspired to use orange as an accent color for the table.

I chose a damask tablecloth in this hue to dress the kitchen up a bit. Several years ago, I loaned out a few pieces of my blue and white collection for a wedding, and as a thank-you gift from the mother of the bride, I received these beautiful dragon napkins.

One of my favorite china patterns is Mottahedeh's "Blue Canton." We use this as our everyday pattern at Chestnut Cottage. (Well, actually, we have several "everyday patterns," and we use them all!) This pattern is noteworthy for its blue lattice border surrounding landscape scenes. The popular Chinese design has also inspired a number of European versions, most notably English stoneware. Blue and white "Canton" or

"Nanking" wares were named for the great Chinese trading ports from which they came. Chinese blue and white porcelain was in demand in the United States well into the nineteenth century and has become a part of the heritage of many American families, mine included. I fondly remember my paternal grandmother's "Blue Willow" pattern and, perhaps, that is what fueled my lifelong love for the color pairing.

As you must have noticed by now, I love a mix of patterns on a table. I recently became fascinated with another Mottahedeh pattern, "Blue Dragon." In ancient China, the dragon was the symbol for the emperor bestowing good fortune. The period of Emperor K'ang Hsi (1662–1722) was one of the high points in the development of blue and white wares.

So many blue patterns I love at Mottahedeh, and so little storage space left at Chestnut Cottage!

I must say that studying the design elements of a china pattern certainly increases the joy of having and using your patterns. I always enjoy chatting with Wendy Kvalheim, President/CEO/Design Director of Mottahedeh China. She has headed the company for the past twenty-five years, although the company has been in business for more than ninety. Recently I had the opportunity to talk with her about the four patterns I used in the Shades of Blue Birthday gathering—"Blue Shou," "Blue Canton," "Blue Dragon," and "Blue Lace." I was especially interested in the "Blue Shou," as it is a relatively new pattern. Wendy told me they took motifs from their iconic "Blue Canton" pattern, enlarged them, and gave the pattern a wider border for a more contemporary look. "Blue Shou" was designed on a white body, rather than on the gray body of "Blue Canton," again making it a bit more contemporary. If you study "Blue Shou," you can spot the enlarged pagoda motif and the more stylized pine trees. "Shou" is the Chinese word for longevity, and the pine tree, a key element of the pattern, symbolizes endurance and long life.

Wendy explained that the V design in the pattern is actually birds in a V formation. The designs of this pattern and of "Blue Canton" are very fascinating to me, and it was a pleasure to hear these design details from the design director herself. Wendy believes that fine china is essential to any menu!

It's a Party!

Join us for a
Birthday Party
honoring

Holli Morris

at noon
on Wednesday, August 18th
Chestnut Cottage
280 Rolling Drive
Waynesville

Please respond to
kathryn@kathryngreeleydesigns.com

I enjoy mixing patterns, and I love to layer the old with the new. A few years ago, one of my college professors willed me the loveliest antique cobalt fish set. I treasure this gift and find great joy in its intricate design details. The set, which includes a master fish platter and eight individual round fish plates, is French Limoges and is marked "CH Field Haviland."

Charles Field Haviland (CH Field Haviland) left America for Limoges in the early 1850s to work for his uncle, David Haviland, founder of Haviland and Company. There, he rented a porcelain factory in partnership with his father and brother. Subsequently, he opened his own porcelain decorating studio and exported items to the United States. He married the granddaughter of Francois Alluad and later took control of the Alluad porcelain factory, one of the oldest Limoges factories.

Charles Field retired in 1881, and the company became known as Gérard, Dufraisseix and Morel using the ware mark GDM. The partners changed around 1890, and the company was thereafter known as Gérard and Dufraisseix—and eventually Gérard, Dufraisseix and Abbot, using the mark GDA. My set is marked in brown with "CH Field Haviland Limoges" inside a double circle and a separate GDM mark. This color of mark was used from 1882–1900. This antique fish set not only complements the new Mottahedeh pieces, but it also inspired the menu for this gathering.

Bamboo cutlery and napkin rings carried through the Chinese design element of the table. I combined these pieces with French Limoges and French opaline stemware. Eight white opaline goblets from the French company Portieux/Vallérysthal stood out against vintage Libby cobalt blown-glass tumblers.

Portieux/Vallérysthal is a glass producer with a complex—and interesting—history. Originally founded in 1836 as Société des Verreries Réunies de Plaine de Walsch et Vallérysthal, the company (in Lorraine, France) became Klenglin et Cie in 1855, and a mix of Bohemian and French glass workers created an array of opaline and decorative glass. In 1870, this area of France became part of Germany for several decades after France lost the Franco-German War. Up to that point, most of Vallérysthal sales had been within France, but when the maps changed and the factory was no longer inside French territory, the company found it difficult to export their glass out of Germany. To get around this problem, they quickly purchased the Portieux glass works operation located in Vosges, France, and while the head office remained in Vallérysthal, they could now export through Portieux. The new name was registered in both French and German and became the Vallérysthal/Portieux brand we still refer to today.

Shades of orange and blue flowers filled a blue and white container and six antique "cricket vases" decorated the birthday table. These intricate little vases are also referred to as brush pots. The vibrant shades of orange in the dahlias confirmed once and for all that all the work I put into the garden was worth every minute!

Across from the table on an antique sideboard, I employed a pair of blue and white vases to hold the lovely, full heads of 'Limelight' hydrangeas.

Shades of Blue
Birthday Menu

Pimm's Cup

Gingered Chicken Cocktail Cakes with Cilantro Lime Mayonnaise

Trio of Trout

Poached Trout with Traditional Cucumber Raita

Smoked Trout Blini Puffs

Smoked Trout Dip

Baby Greens with Grilled Peaches and
Baked Goat Cheese Rounds with Balsamic Vinaigrette

Tomato Basil Tart

"Blue Canton" Birthday Cake

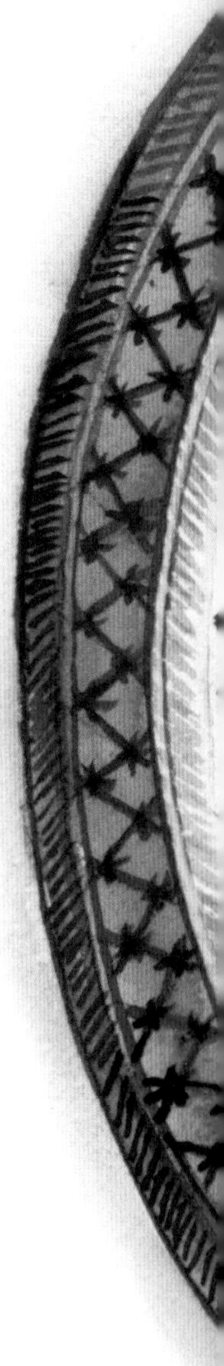

We started our little celebration with one of our favorite summer drinks, Pimm's Cup, which I served in the library.

Cheers to this thirst-quenching, supremely summer drink!

Pimm's No. 1, the drink's namesake and key ingredient, is a gin-based liqueur created in 1823 by James Pimm, a farmer's son from Kent who ran an oyster house near the Bank of England in London. Pimm's Cup, which features the light flavors of cucumber, orange, and fresh mint, made its debut in 1840 in London as a health drink. For many, the refreshing concoction was (and is) a welcome relief from summer heat. The drink quickly grew in popularity after it began to be sold commercially by 1859—and, as they say, the rest is history! You may know Pimm's Cup as a favorite cooler at Wimbledon. With a rather heavy lunch on the menu, I opted for bite-size Gingered Chicken Cocktail Cakes to serve alongside our Pimm's Cup.

One of the entertaining truths I live by is designing menus with locally sourced, seasonal foods. I am so inspired by the variety of delicious local food offerings available, and they guide the composition of my menus, as you'll notice throughout this book. Using local foods whenever possible supports local food producers and vendors, and since most of these producers and vendors use sustainable practices, using their products is another win for everyone. At the Mother's Day Luncheon, I served a wonderful local goat cheese from Dark Cove Farms, and it makes an appearance at this birthday event, too.

Another local source I use frequently for both special occasions and in my everyday cooking is Sunburst Trout Farm. For over seventy years, three generations of the same family have successfully maintained this innovative rainbow trout enterprise. They have perfected their cold, smoked Scottish trout, and I use it in the blini puffs on this birthday menu along with their award-winning trout caviar. Many people may not know that freshwater caviar is a true delicacy, with a pleasing, mild flavor. Their trout fillets have a pinkish color and are so plump you might think they are salmon. If I've made your mouth water and you don't live in Western North Carolina, the good news is Sunburst offers an online store and is widely seen on fine restaurant menus across the country.

Because I can't seem to get enough of Sunburst's products, I used their trout fillet for the poached trout on the menu and their smoked trout for the trout dip.

Smoked Trout and Caviar Blini Puffs

INGREDIENTS

For the Puffs

2 cups cottage cheese

1 tablespoon sour cream

1 teaspoon pure vanilla extract

½ teaspoon granulated sugar

3 tablespoons unsalted butter, melted

3 eggs

½ cup all-purpose flour

For the Garnish

1 cup crème fraîche

4 ounces cold smoked trout

2 ounces trout caviar

PREPARATION

Preheat oven to 350 degrees. Place cottage cheese, sour cream, vanilla extract, sugar, butter, eggs, and flour in the bowl of a food processor and blend until smooth.

Pour the batter into 24 greased mini muffin pans and bake for 12–15 minutes or until golden brown. Cool on a cooling rack. The puffs tend to fall in the middle, so don't become alarmed if this happens! The puffs may be made ahead of time and reheated for 5 minutes at 350 degrees.

ASSEMBLING THE PUFFS

When puffs are cool, spoon a small amount of crème fraîche onto each blini and top with a slice of smoked trout or a small amount of caviar.

This recipe makes 24 puffs.

Smoked Trout Dip

INGREDIENTS

5 ounces boneless smoked trout fillets

½ cup cream cheese

½ cup sour cream

2 tablespoons fresh chives, chopped

1 tablespoon fresh-squeezed lemon juice

Kosher salt

Fresh-ground black pepper

PREPARATION

Flake the boneless smoked trout into small pieces with a fork and mash with a fork until finely shredded. Add the remaining ingredients and mix until creamy. Salt and pepper to taste. You will probably need very little salt.

Serve with crackers or crisp vegetables for dipping. I love this dip on the blinis.

Note: This recipe is flexible! You can swap scallions or minced red onions for chives; mascarpone for cream cheese; or Greek yogurt for sour cream. Add a dash of horseradish or Tabasco for zip, but use a light hand so the trout can shine!

To showcase and contrast the local trout products, I decided to follow them with baby greens with grilled peaches and goat cheese rounds, along with a Tomato Basil Tart. I really only enjoy peaches and tomatoes when they are in season, so I always look forward to summer when they are locally available.

The Tomato Basil Tart (commonly known at Chestnut Cottage as tomato pie!) is one of my summer favorites. With loads of fresh basil in the garden and heirloom tomatoes at the farmer's market, it seemed to be a perfect addition to the birthday menu. While it may not be the most perfect-looking pie, I think you will find the combination of tomatoes, basil, cheese, and Vidalia onions irresistible to your palate.

Tomato Basil Tart

INGREDIENTS

1 refrigerator piecrust, unbaked

1½ cups shredded mozzarella cheese, divided

6 Roma tomatoes or 4 medium heirloom tomatoes

½ onion, sliced

1 cup fresh basil leaves, cut into thin strips (chiffonade)

4 cloves garlic, peeled and chopped fine

½ cup mayonnaise

¼ cup grated Parmesan cheese

⅛ teaspoon black pepper

1 teaspoon olive oil

PREPARATION

Preheat oven to 450 degrees. Place the piecrust in a 9-inch tart pan or pie plate. Prick the bottom and lower sides of the pastry shell. Bake for about 8 minutes until the shell is lightly browned. Remove from the oven and immediately sprinkle ½ cup of the mozzarella cheese on the bottom of the shell. This helps to seal the crust and prevent it from getting soggy.

Mix together the remaining 1 cup of mozzarella with the mayonnaise, Parmesan, garlic, and pepper. Set aside. Slice the tomatoes and press between two paper towels to remove excess moisture. Lightly sauté the onions in 1 teaspoon of olive oil.

ASSEMBLING THE TART

Arrange the tomatoes evenly on the melted cheese in the pastry shell. Add the onion and basil. Evenly spread the cheese mixture to the edges.

Bake at 375 degrees for 35–40 minutes or until the top is golden.

Note: I use pie weights during the crust's first bake to avoid shrinkage of the pastry, and I cover the edges of the crust with aluminum foil, so they don't get too brown. When using heirloom tomatoes for this tart, my favorites are a combination of Cherokee Purple and Mr. Stripey.

The perfect ending to the birthday meal was a "Blue Canton" birthday cake. Expert cake maker Callie Stingel never batted an eye when I said I wanted the cake to look just like the "Blue Canton" china pattern. Not only are her cakes beautiful, but they are also very delicious!

I always opt for her white cake with almond filling and almond buttercream icing. These cakes are a favorite of mine and the birthday girl's—so I knew it would be perfect for her celebration.

When I recently visited the Mottahedeh showroom in High Point, North Carolina, I was quite taken by an addition to their "Blue Lace" pattern. As you see, I simply couldn't resist the small individual cake stands for this luncheon.

After enjoying our cake, I gave our guests a set of the blue and white cocktail napkins that repeated the "Blue Canton" theme.

Collecting

Blue and White, Copper, and Menus

As you know, Holli, the birthday girl, and I share a love of collecting blue and white. It is such a timeless color combination, and I have collected it for over fifty years. I have never grown tired of my blue and white collection, and I continue to add special pieces. Many of these live in the kitchen at Chestnut Cottage, and we were surrounded by it at her birthday lunch.

When I was designing my kitchen, I found the Faïence Blue Tile Collection from Country Floors and mounted the wine merchant, cheese merchant, and bread merchant tiles behind my sixty-inch range.

I never cease to enjoy these three merchants while I am cooking. And what else does one need other than wine, cheese, and bread?

Some of my blue and white pieces are somewhat more "precious" than others. I collect finds that are in good condition and that speak to me. Because I have been collecting for so long, I need to maximize display space in the kitchen: Dressers and recessed shelves hold pieces that are not only treasured, but also used daily.

When I purchased the cottage, I was pleased to find this recessed shelving and later added some clay plumbing tiles for wine storage.

I've got a few other characters in my collection as well. For example, I can't help but chuckle when I look up and find the little "nodder" having a cup of tea and agreeing with any gossip she might hear in the kitchen. Doesn't she look smug?

As I look at each piece, I fondly remember where I found it or who gave it to me as a gift.

For example, it was none other than the birthday girl, Holli Morris, who gifted me this "Blue Willow" divided dish that I use regularly.

Years ago, a very special client gave me two tiny tea sets in blue and white.

I was hopeful that I might be blessed with a little granddaughter to enjoy these tea sets with, but alas, only two cute grandsons!

Another sweet client gave me the blue and white Westie plate, which lives behind a fun little gin decanter.

While in a tavern in Yorkshire, England, I spotted this piece behind the bar. After using all of my Southern charm, the bartender finally gifted it to me so that I would fondly remember his bar.

A combination of Flow Blue and blue and white transferware crowns the kitchen windows. Here it is within reach for everyday use, where it also lives in compatibility with vintage cobalt glass.

Cobalt glass was first produced during the Depression era, from the 1930s into the early 1940s. Both the Hazel-Atlas Glass Company and the Fenton Glass Company were pioneers in the production of this lovely glass. Its deep-blue color is achieved by incorporating the cobalt oxide element into molten glass. I can assure you the cobalt beehive vases on the top shelf are taken down and used regularly!

My blue and white collection is primarily Flow Blue, but it encompasses a wide variety of sources, styles, and time periods. Flow Blue has been one of my most enduring passions for many years. This earthenware (most of which was transferware) was first created in England

in the early-to-mid 1800s as a sturdier, less expensive alternative to Chinese porcelain. The technique used to make it quickly became popular with English potters for two reasons: the ease of transferring the printed, under-glaze designs and the fact that the "flowing" of the blue on the transfers hid most imperfections in the vessel. The "flow" in these patterns was created by introducing lime into the firing process. Once added, it gave the patterns a fastness and the signature hazy, "melt-away" look that makes Flow Blue so famous.

The production of Flow Blue eventually spread from England to France, and then on to Germany, Holland, and eventually America. It took its place as an affordable alternative to porcelain since it was delicate and fine enough to use at formal dinner parties. While some English critics of Flow Blue were harsh and unforgiving of the technique, the American public took an instant liking to the patterns, colors, and, of course, the price point. By the late nineteenth century, it could be found in the homes of many Americans, regardless of their economic or social status.

The production of Flow Blue ended early in the twentieth century, so no matter which pattern you find, you know your piece is at least a century old—making it an antique. Be sure to look for a maker's mark on the underside of a piece. The marks are fascinating to study, and they tell the who, when, and where of each specific piece. There are many books dedicated to the identification of marks if you want to trace the history of a piece you have.

My collection also includes many pieces of "Blue Willow" transferware. The "Blue Willow" pattern is said to be the most collected china pattern ever made,

and you will find it throughout Chestnut Cottage. Transferware gets its name from the printing method used to produce its unique look. In this process, tissue paper is laid atop engraved copper plates that are covered with a film of cobalt oxide. My love affair with it began as a young child at my paternal grandmother's home. She treasured her "Blue Willow," which was likely purchased at the local five-and-dime, and our family enjoyed many years of delicious meals on this humble pattern.

Perhaps one of my most valuable pieces is a Flow Blue toast rack. I hunted for this piece for years, and one Christmas, I found it under the tree. A favorite antique dealer located it, contacted Wells, and now it sits between two lovely spill vases in an English dresser!

On one kitchen wall, I framed groupings of blue and white with hand-painted trees that have airy blue leaves.

As you know by now, you'll find blue and white collections throughout the cottage, and a favorite piece of Flow Blue is a sturdy, chairside fern stand that lives in our keeping room.

I use the fern stand for piles of books occasionally topped with a vase of flowers from the garden. In almost every room of Chestnut Cottage, you'll find the walls—and some decorative bracket shelves—are covered with more groupings of my beloved collection.

Secretaries and bookcases find themselves filled with blue and white treasures, and the pieces truly bring me great pleasure no matter what space they are in.

Duncan even likes to surround himself with blue and white! To say that I am an incurable collector of many things would indeed be an understatement. The blue and white collection is extensive. However, there is always room for smaller collections that can be woven in alongside these pieces . . . well, most of the time!

One of these smaller collections began when I found a much-loved old copper fish poacher.

Then there was the samovar, and next came the little rectangular teapot. And just like that, I was collecting copperware.

Watering cans, pots, pans, and copper molds seemed to follow.

Much like the blue and white collection, I buy pieces that are in good condition and speak to me—and all are regularly in use at Chestnut Cottage.

A few years ago, on a trip to Bordeaux, France, I fell in love with a small French pastry. It was flavored with rum and vanilla and had a soft and tender custard center on a dark, thick, caramelized crust. I came to find out they were called *canelés*. It's hard to know for sure, but perhaps some of my love for this Bordeaux specialty wasn't just about the taste. It was also likely the small copper cylinders in which they are baked! I simply couldn't leave Bordeaux without a few of these copper canelé molds.

Once I was back home, the pressure was on to perfect this rather complicated delicacy. I must confess that I was very intimidated by the recipes I found but finally decided I should just jump in and see what happened. Traditionally, the molds are brushed with beeswax and butter, so I ordered beeswax and assembled my ingredients. The ingredients are a simple combination of vanilla, rum, eggs, butter, sugar, and flour. But, believe me, there is nothing simple about the process. My first results were most humbling! I set about compiling several recipes and after reading and re-reading them for what seemed to be 100 times, I told myself it was time to just do it!

Oh, what toil and trouble a little addition to the copper collection can bring!

But, oh, what joy lives in these little morsels that are like nothing I had ever tasted. Even though they haven't been perfect every time, I have been pleased with my canelé results. And perfect or not, it's interesting to note that they *always* disappear not long after being placed on the cooling rack! The rich, moist, custardy interior sealed with a crispy, caramelized shell almost seems like crème brûlée in a crust! I might add that canelés are most delightful with a nice glass of rosé champagne.

One of Wells's favorite collections at Chestnut Cottage are his antique corkscrews. Opening the Leader of the Pack wine bottles with these corkscrews proved to be an interesting task for our guests and provided us with a few very good laughs.

To determine if a corkscrew is valuable, you will want to consider three important factors: its rarity, its desirability, and its condition. There are most definitely rare corkscrews out there, but for our collecting purposes, desirability and condition are the most important factors.

It's not certain when the first corkscrews were made, but it's thought to have been sometime during the mid-seventeenth century in England. Early versions were mostly a simple T shape and were designed for direct pull. As demand increased, more interesting shapes evolved, all of which had mechanical advantages over the T design.

The first corkscrew patent was awarded in England in 1795 to Reverend Samuel Henshall of Oxford, and hundreds of British designs have been produced in the 200+ years since. The British, French, Italians, and Americans stand out as being the most prolific in both design and manufacture, and among their wares, you'll find designs that are good, designs that are bad, and designs that are very perfectly hopeless in removing a cork!

While there are literally thousands of different types of corkscrews you can collect, I have purchased most of Wells's small collection at antique shows. You'll find them in a multitude of materials from ore to iron to boxwood and rosewood brass, to mention a few. My favorite of his collection is the brass and bone corkscrew with a brush at the top which is a Victorian Dowler Thomason-type corkscrew. I also love the vintage solid brass French Sanbri corker.

We have several of the T-type corkscrews: one with a wooden top that has a brush on the end and another that has an interesting wooden case at the bottom. You don't see them on modern corkscrews, but many from the late eighteenth and early to mid-nineteenth centuries often had stiff bristles on one end. These so-called dusting brushes were used to remove debris from the wax used to help seal the bottle (which was more common than it is now) or any dust or fungus that might have accumulated on the cork.

Wells chuckled when he learned that a corkscrew collector is called a *helixophile*. He said his humble little collection of corkscrews hardly qualified him for such an elaborate moniker! And if nothing else, his little collection is always a great conversation topic!

Summer is seen by many as a good time to travel, but I would argue to the contrary! Most *any time* of the year is a good time to travel! I love to explore new places, and I have been fortunate to have been able to travel extensively over the years—often for work and more often for pleasure. My menu collection at the cottage is the one collection that especially documents our travels.

Early on in my adult life, I began to notice the interesting designs and colors of the menus in places we dined. I thought, *Wouldn't these be an interesting design element!*

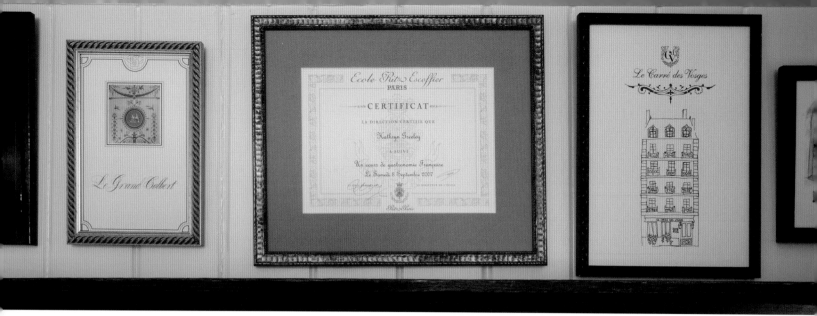

So, at some point, I started using my best Southern charm (again) to ask if I could take my menus home with me. This worked beautifully at most places, but others were not so hospitable, and even unpleasant enough that I don't want to document the experience! I will confess that if I really, *really* wanted the menu and was told no, I carefully slipped out with it either under my coat or tucked into some other creative place!

My perseverance proved to be fruitful, and before long, I was decorating the hall between the kitchen and the master bedroom with menus from around the world. As I passed down this hall, I took myself back to Ireland, England, Scotland, New York, Spain, and so many other interesting destinations—if only for a moment. But at one point, when my menu collecting really became a passion, I realized my hallway was not going to be as large as I needed, and I started displaying them on doors, above doors, and anyplace else I could find an empty spot.

In among the menus, I have tucked in my certificate from The Ritz Cooking School in Paris.

I was with a group of designer friends on that trip, which made it that much more memorable.

Come with me down the hall to some of my favorite dining experiences.

There was Banks Restaurant in London before the theater . . .

And No. 27—The Green at the Shelbourne Hotel in Dublin . . .

And Read's in Mallorca, Spain.

D'Arcy's Tavern in County Kerry, Ireland.

The Ballymaloe House in County Cork, Ireland.

And The Goring in London.

And The Portaferry Hotel in County Down, Ireland, a lovely hotel only a few miles from my maternal grandfather's homeplace!

La Grenouille and Swifty's in New York.

And many others.

Read's

d'Arcy's
RESTAURANT

"...let me fix you a Martini that's pure magic. It may not make life's problems disappear, but it'll certainly reduce their size." -- Some Came Running, 1959 Frank Sinatra/Dean Martin

"The only green vegetables I get are Martini olives." -- B. F. Pierce (M.A.S.H.)

"Twas a woman who drove me to drink, and I never had the courtesy to thank her for it." -- W. C. Fields

The Ritz-Carlton, Naples

Martini Menu

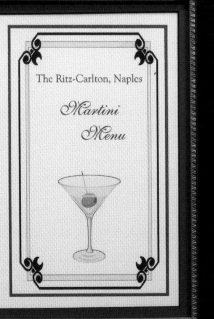

This menu collection is a favorite of mine and also of many visitors who come to Chestnut Cottage. I can verify that every single one of the menus has a story to tell! For example, while Wells and I were enjoying our dinner in the Goring Hotel restaurant, a party was seated at the next table. The woman said hello in a polite, reserved way, and I returned the greeting. Wells leaned over and said, "Do you know that woman?" I looked at him and replied, "Yes, I do. It's Margaret Thatcher, the Prime Minister!"

Simple Pleasures

DINNER FOR TWO AND CANNING

Summer, like every other season, has its own simple pleasures. I personally enjoy preserving and canning at this time of year—especially strawberry jam, my special lime pickles, and green beans. It involves hard work, but I find the whole process a very satisfying endeavor and would certainly consider it a simple pleasure. And I do have to admit that after several days of standing over the jars and canners, it's marvelous to plan a simple dinner for two in the garden to relax.

We have a little outdoor stone fireplace in the upper garden that was here when I purchased the cottage. I have always been rather fascinated with this structure, and it is a perfect spot for lunch or a small dinner gathering. In the mountains, summer evenings can be chilly, so a little fire brings a cozy feeling to the meal. On a path up to the fireplace area, you can sit on the bench with a miniature stone English cottage.

You already know that I simply can't resist beautiful fabrics, so when I came across Brunschwig and Fils's "Zenobia" linen print, I knew just how I would use it at the cottage: I would make a tablecloth! I love the depth and range of the blues and greens, and I thought it would be perfect with any of my blue and white china patterns. For this particular dinner, I chose Spode's "Tower Blue" china pattern. I purchased many pieces of this pattern at an unbelievable price at an antique shop (formerly an old schoolhouse) on the way to my lake house that was going out of business. I divided the pieces between Chatuge Cottage and Chestnut Cottage.

This pattern was made by Spode at two different times and—as with many collectibles and dinnerware—the maker's mark helps to date when pieces were made. Mine is the older mark, indicating it was produced from 1902 until 1970. The newer marked pieces were made from 1970 to 2005, when the pattern was discontinued.

I combined my Alain Saint-Joanis flatware with the Spode china, and the contrast of the rosewood with the china and fabric seemed just right for outdoor dining. The pattern, "Montana Rosewood" from their Tendance Collection, is made in workshops in La Monnerie, France. I was rather shocked to learn that it is dishwasher safe. However, it will never see the inside of the dishwasher at Chestnut Cottage! Something this beautiful deserves to be washed by hand.

My workroom had just enough fabric left after making the tablecloth to make four napkins for myself, which I then monogrammed with a simple "G." With a few daisies, phlox, ferns, and hostas close by in the garden for a quick little table arrangement, what could be better than a grilled pork tenderloin, a simple zucchini casserole, and a glass of wine on a summer's evening?

L ike all good things, summer must come to a close. And, by Labor Day, I must say I'm already looking ahead to crisp fall mornings. As the leaves begin to change and the days become cooler, I don't mind spending a little extra time in the kitchen, especially when baking is involved. The days of September and October have me ready to whip up a fresh apple cake and even get a jumpstart on making the zucchini bread I traditionally give at Christmastime. I hope you'll join me for all the pleasures of autumn that await at Chestnut Cottage.

Autumn

"There is a beautiful spirit breathing now
Its mellow richness on the clustered trees,
And from a beaker full of richest dyes
Pouring new glory on the autumn woods."

—HENRY WADSWORTH LONGFELLOW

"It's the first day of autumn! A time of hot chocolatey mornings and toasty marshmallow evenings, and, best of all, leaping into leaves!"

—WINNIE THE POOH

In the Garden

Autumn in the mountains brings us crisp mornings and sunny afternoons with azure-blue skies. Shades of bronze and gold mingle with scarlet and rust and peach. The garden becomes a glorious patchwork of autumn color.

Dahlias continue to bloom well into the fall here, and I fill the cottage with bouquets.

The Joe-Pye keeps company with the dahlias, and several spring flowers decide to show off again.

Random white irises and a few delphiniums offer sweet surprises on an autumn morning. The old, elegant oaks start to dress in autumn hues that range from copper to yellow, and the winterberry bushes are full of beautiful red berries. I can't bear to see the birds feasting on these beautiful berries, so I cover them with bird netting in hopes that their beauty will last through the season—for holiday decorating!

It may come as no surprise that I always get a bit sad when the autumn garden begins to fade. But before it goes down for its winter nap, I have an abundance of autumn chores to be done!

AUTUMN GARDEN CHORES

Before the first frost, plant any new
perennials I want to add to the borders.

After the first frost, cut back all the perennials, collect their
seed heads, and disperse the seeds throughout the borders.

Do the autumn fertilization.

Gather all the millions of leaves the old oak trees have dropped.
This is perhaps the most time-consuming autumn chore!

Place netting over the winterberry bushes to prevent the
birds from stealing the beautiful scarlet-red berries!

Close up the fountain ahead of winter.

Then it's back to the dahlias!

We routinely plant our dahlias straight in the ground in their nursery pots. After the first frost, I remove the pots to prepare the tubers for winter storage. If you plant dahlias in the ground, I recommend using a pitchfork to loosen the soil around them first, so you don't damage the tubers which grow under the ground. In either case, first trim the stems back to about six inches in length so that you can more easily handle the tubers. Remove the trimmed plants and rinse their tubers with water or brush off the dirt with a medium-size bristle brush. I remove any rotten or soft spots and place each tuber in a separate paper bag so they can dry.

After a week or so, I transfer them to a box or crate that stays in the potting shed over the winter. One of the tiny garages built in 1925 at Chestnut Cottage serves beautifully as our potting shed. It is definitely too small for any car that you might find here, but it makes for a perfect potting and gardening shed. In the spring, I will divide the tubers and plant them back in the nursery pots. The tubers seem to like temperatures between 40 and 50 degrees for their winter rest, and the shed provides just that!

One very special addition to the property are three tiny chestnut seedlings. The American Chestnut Society in Asheville, North Carolina, gifted them to us, and we planted them in the woods behind the cottage. We caged them to keep the wildlife away until they can survive on their own. It's exciting to watch these seedlings grow, and I am hoping they will make chestnut trees for future generations!

Since I don't have any grown chestnut trees at the cottage, in early fall I visit my friend Holli's garden on nearby Chinquapin Lane where I gather plenty for a table arrangement at the cottage.

Nature's details are simply incredible, and when the chestnut burrs open to reveal the actual nut, they look like tiny birds with open mouths!

Nature designed these burrs to make them impervious to predators. Believe me: a thick pair of gloves are necessary when you're gathering them!

Gatherings

Dreaming of Tuscany

If you've ever experienced Tuscan, you'll always be
"Dreaming of Tuscany"

Join me for a night of
reminiscing, Tuscan food and wine, and friendship

Saturday, October 16th at 6:00 pm
Chestnut Cottage
280 Rolling Drive
Waynesville

Please respond to
kathryn@kathryngreeleydesigns.com

Dreaming of Tuscany Menu

Antipasto Misto

Caprese Tomato Salad

Tagliatelle with Ragu di Carne

Limoncello Sorbet

Roast Pork Tenderloin with Olive Picatta Sauce

Tuscan Style White Beans with Fresh Sage

Apple Tart with Rosemary

A few years ago, my close friend Anne Underwood invited me and six other friends to join her for ten days in Italy to celebrate a "significant" birthday! It was such a lovely surprise to be included, and plans were quickly set in motion when she rented a beautiful villa near Montalcino. We flew into Pisa and started our journey to the villa. After some difficulty (for a group of American women trying to "turn at the correct cypress tree") I decided to knock on the door of a random villa to ask directions. We finally arrived at Villa Fontanelle—having been led there by a handsome, silver-haired Italian who answered the door. Villa Fontanelle is owned by interior designer Piero Castellini from Milan. From the first moment, the architecture and interiors were so inspiring that I couldn't stop thinking about designing and planning a Tuscan event back at Chestnut Cottage.

Our days were filled with lazy hours spent reading and chatting around the villa's lovely pool and terrace, wine tastings, antiquing, and shopping for exquisite local dinnerware and linens. A few of us even wandered off to go to the Badia a Coltibuono cooking school that stands in a vineyard in the upper woodlands of the Chianti region, just south of Siena. Badia a Coltibuono is housed inside an ancient monastery built by Benedictine monks in the eleventh century, and the name means the "abbey of good harvest." It was a perfect place to indulge our passions for food and wine while we learned new cooking techniques and recipes.

Inspired by the trip, I recently decided to host a dinner for these same traveling companions to reminisce about our glorious time. During many of the nights at the villa, we dined by candlelight on a stone terrace. I thought it would be fun to try and recreate our dining experiences on the upper terrace at Chestnut Cottage. Being a designer meant that I had to procure a nice Italian-style table, some chairs—and lots of candles. Village Antiques in Asheville graciously loaned me a very lovely table and an antique set of leather chairs. When I strung lights in the trees, a festive mood set in. While the view from our terrace in North Carolina can't quite compete with the one at the villa, a table abundant with flowers, candles, and Italian dinnerware invited us to imagine that we were once again about to sit down to *cena* there. To get things going, I set a small garden table next to the fountain in the garden and covered it with a lovely tablecloth that I purchased in Montalcino on our trip.

Our evening began with Prosecco cocktails made with a splash of Campari and garnished with rosemary and blackberries. I served them with an antipasto misto.

We enjoyed the crisp autumn evening and then proceeded to the back terrace where the table was ready for a hearty Tuscan meal!

If you've ever experienced this magical place, you'll always be dreaming of Tuscany!

Table Inspiration

Dinnerware found in a tiny pottery shop in Florence was my table inspiration for this special event. The pattern—in cobalt and mustard—completely suited this lover of all things blue and white! The somewhat rustic feel of the pattern made it a perfect choice for a Tuscan dinner party.

I love how its shades of blue are accented with berries in mustard, copper, and wine—all with vivid green leaves. Each piece is signed in dark cobalt.

Dreaming of Tuscany

Antipasto Misto

Caprese Tomato Salad

Tagliatelle with Ragu di Carne

Limoncello Sorbet

Roast Pork Tenderloin with
Olive-Picatta Sauce

Tuscan Style White Beans
with Fresh Sage

Apple Tart with Rosemary

Dreaming of Tuscany

Antipasto Misto

Caprese Tomato Salad

Tagliatelle with Ragù di Carne

Limoncello Sorbet

Roast Pork Tenderloin with
Olive-Picatta Sauce

Tuscan Style White Beans
with Fresh Sage

Apple Tart with Rosemary

The Italian-style table had an intricate parquet tabletop, so I chose dark-blue woven placemats to allow the beauty of the wood to shine through. Again, I used the lovely Alain Saint-Joanis cutlery with the twisted rosewood handles.

A mix of William Yeoward "Fanny" water goblets in blue and Saint Louis "Tommy" wine glasses framed each place setting.

We served one of our favorite wines from Montalcino—a 2016 vintage Castiglion del Bosco Brunello di Montalcino. I purchased handmade pottery vases by Vicki Miller in a soft shade of mustard at Vivianne Metzger Antiques. They looked beautiful holding sunflowers, a variety of dahlias and hypericum, and a mix of bay leaf and olive branch greens. The flowers really pulled out the wines, golds, white, and greens in the pottery dinnerware.

I have collected barley twist candlesticks for many years, and I have never grown tired of them. I use the collection throughout Chestnut Cottage, very often on the tabletops when I entertain. Here, I wove the candlesticks in among the pottery vases filled with autumn flowers. I love how their design is complemented by the handles on the Alain Saint-Joanis cutlery.

As we lingered into the evening, the candles provided a wonderful atmosphere for reminiscing and drinking good Italian wine! We dined by a lovely music collection, *Tuscany: A Romantic Journey*, which included beautiful orchestral recordings of Italian classics. I used our French wine-tasting table to serve a family-style Tuscan meal. It lives in Wells's wine cellar most of the time, but it is light enough to carry anywhere in the cottage or even outside for alfresco dining. Originally used in nineteenth-century France, these tables were kept in wine cellars where space was limited. When wine tasters arrived or the harvest was in and wine needed to be sampled, the tabletops were flipped down and pressed into use to hold bottles, glasses, and other wine-tasting accessories. I highly recommend investing in a table of this size and type. It's perfect for a multitude of uses.

The menu on this particular night included a caprese salad, tagliatelle with *ragu di carne*, and limoncello sorbet.

I also served roast pork tenderloin with an olive picatta sauce.

Tuscan-style white beans with fresh sage, and crusty Italian bread rounded out the menu.

One of my favorite discoveries in Tuscany was balsamic pearls! They add a burst of flavor to the caprese salad—or to any salad for that matter! When a mixture of balsamic vinegar and agar is added by drops into cold olive oil, it sinks into the thicker, colder medium, and the agar encases the droplets of balsamic, which creates the pearls. The pearls allow the balsamic to hold its flavor. If you just drizzled the dressing over the salad, the flavor would become diluted. The pearls provide a concentrated hit of that beautiful flavor.

The same can be said for the mozzarella pearls and the basil. My favorite dish of the evening was the tagliatelle with *ragu di carne*. The following recipe is a combination of recipes from friends, the cooking school in Tuscany, and my own tweaks! Lots of ingredients, but lots of taste!

Tagliatelle with Ragu di Carne

INGREDIENTS

1 cup white or yellow onion, diced

2 cloves garlic, minced

1 carrot, finely chopped

½ pound ground chuck

½ pound ground veal

1 pound ground Italian sausage

¼ cup melted butter

1 tablespoon olive oil

½ pound fresh mushrooms, chopped

¾ cup diced celery

½ cup diced green pepper

1 28-ounce can Italian-style
    crushed tomatoes (I use the
    San Marzano brand)

1 12-ounce can tomato paste

½ cup dry red wine

1 tablespoon granulated sugar

1½ teaspoon Angostura bitters

1½ teaspoon Worcestershire Sauce

½ teaspoon celery salt

¼ teaspoon ground black pepper

Dash of ground red pepper

1 teaspoon dried oregano

½ teaspoon dried thyme

½ teaspoon dried basil

½ teaspoon dried Italian seasoning

½ teaspoon dried fennel seeds

2 bay leaves

1 8.82-ounce box of Cipriani Tagliatelle

Shaved Parmesan cheese for topping

PREPARATION

Add the onion, garlic, carrot, chuck, veal, and sausage to the butter and olive oil in a large Dutch oven. Place over medium heat and cook until the meat is browned, stirring to crumble. Drain. Add the mushrooms and the next 17 ingredients and bring to a low boil. Reduce heat and simmer uncovered for about 1 hour. Discard the bay leaves.

Cook tagliatelle according to package directions. Drain pasta and transfer to a serving platter. Spoon the sauce over the cooked pasta. Top with shaved Parmesan cheese.

We ended the evening with a real autumn dessert that I have been making for years at Chestnut Cottage. This apple tart, made entirely in the food processor and with fresh apples, is a dessert that always brings rave reviews! While on the trip to Tuscany, I ordered a similar apple tart that had a very interesting flavor—rosemary! So I decided to add a bit of my fresh rosemary to both the crust and the filling. I think it adds a complex flavor that complements the apples in an evocative, delicious way. As dessert was served, I added a very special pair of candles to a pair of the wooden candlesticks to illuminate the flowers and the apple tart.

These interesting candles were a gift from Mary Woltz and her husband, Rob Calvert. Mary's brother, our friend Thomas Woltz, introduced us to Mary's honey and her business, Bees' Needs. Rob collected the wax and bought beautiful molds to make these lovely beeswax candles, whose honey color is the natural color of pure beeswax. Rob removes the frames from the hives, cleans the wax, and melts it down to make the candles, which were such a lovely, meaningful addition to our evening!

Mary is a professional beekeeper with 100 hives on various organic farms at the eastern end of Long Island. She only harvests enough honey from her hives to make sure that the remaining honey will meet the bees' needs. Bees need honey to last the winter, as they consume it for energy as they generate heat by flapping their wings. She carries three types. Early Harvest, also called Marvelous May, is primarily made from the nectar from the black locust tree. It's light with a delicate flavor. The Middle Harvest, also called Juicy July, contains nectar from privet, sunflower, and linden. The Late Harvest, or Fabulous Fall, may contain goldenrod, Japanese knotweed, asters, and occasionally buckwheat, creating a darker, more flavorful honey.

Wells hides Mary's honey, so I rarely get more than a small taste. He believes that Mary's honey is much like a fine wine, with complex notes, and he tries to keep it stowed away for his own pleasure! Mary has won the Good Food Award six times for this lovely honey that Wells keeps hidden!

So many memories, so much friendship, and so many thanks to Anne for the lovely, memorable trip!

"Why would you be anywhere else when you can be in Italy."

—EDITH WHARTON

Apple Tart

INGREDIENTS

For the Pastry

½ cup unsalted butter, cold and cut
into ½-inch pieces

1 cup all-purpose flour

2 tablespoons granulated sugar

¼ teaspoon salt

¼ teaspoon fresh rosemary, chopped

1 tablespoon white vinegar

For the Filling

5–6 apples, peeled and cored
(I use Red Delicious)

¾ cup granulated sugar

2 tablespoons all-purpose flour

1 teaspoon ground cinnamon

¼ teaspoon fresh rosemary needles,
chopped (tender green sprigs only;
no stems)

1 cup chopped pecans (hazelnuts or
almonds would, of course, be more
likely in Italy!)

Whipped cream for topping

PREPARATION

Preheat oven to 400 degrees.

Position the knife blade in the processor
bowl. Add the butter, flour, sugar, salt, and
rosemary. Process 10–15 seconds or until
the mixture resembles coarse meal. With
the processor running, pour vinegar through
the food chute and process 15–20 seconds
or until the dough forms a ball. Remove
dough and press into the bottom and sides
of a 10-inch tart pan with a removable bottom. Set aside.

Cut peeled apples into quarters. Position
the shredding blade in the processor bowl.
Insert apples and shred. Add 3 cups of
shredded apples to the sugar, flour, cinnamon, and rosemary. Mix well. Spoon the
apple mixture evenly into the prepared pastry crust and top with the chopped pecans.
Bake for 45 minutes. Cool and remove side
of tart pan. Cut into slices and top each slice
with whipped cream if desired.

Cheers to Tuscany!

Autumn is a very busy entertaining season at Chestnut Cottage. In November, it is time to organize the big Thanksgiving dinner for family and friends. And as soon as Thanksgiving is over, it's time to celebrate the birthday of one of my favorite individuals!

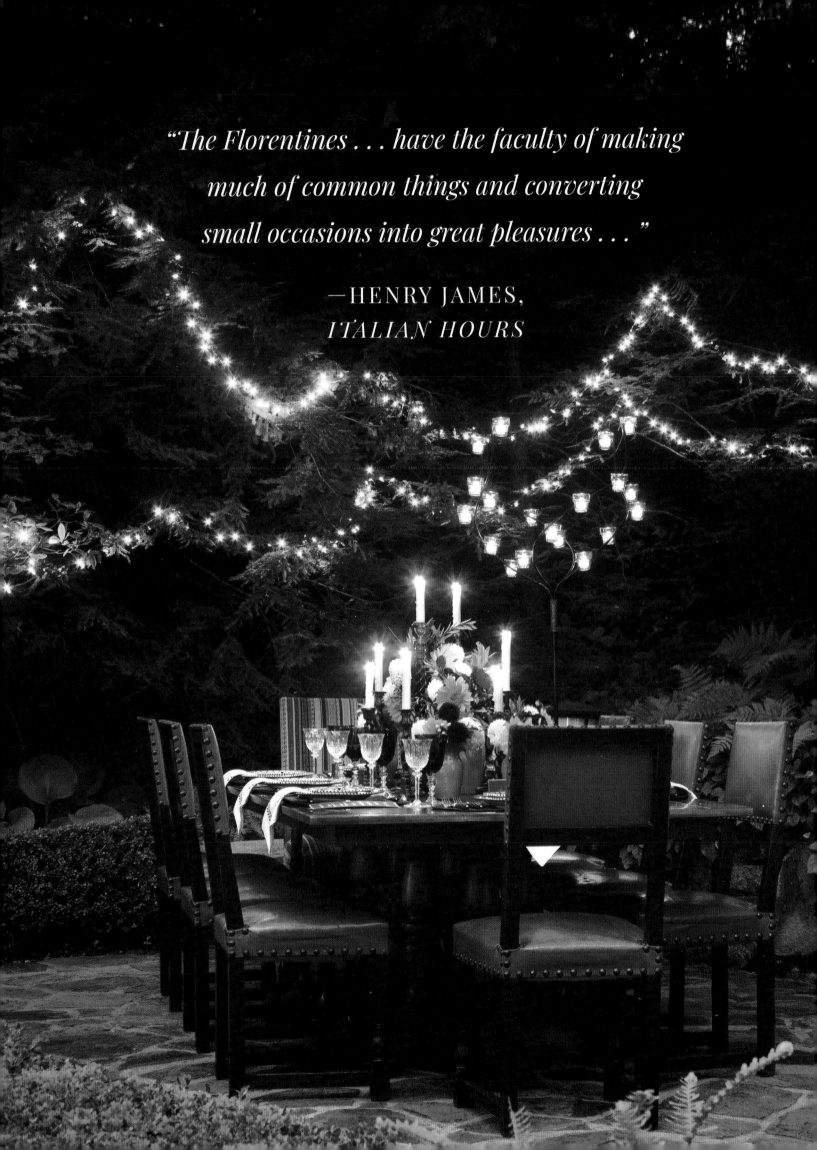

"The Florentines . . . have the faculty of making much of common things and converting small occasions into great pleasures . . . "

—HENRY JAMES,
ITALIAN HOURS

Birthday Blitz— Celebrating Winston Churchill

Birthday Blitz—Celebrating Winston Churchill Menu

Filet of Dover Sole Wrapped in Smoked Salmon

Roast Beef with Yorkshire Pudding

English Peas

Pecorino-Garlic Duchess Potatoes

English Trifle

English Cheese and Fresh Pears

If I could meet one person in history, aside from Jesus, I would want to meet Winston Churchill. I have a nice collection of books about him, and I am fascinated with the story of his life.

One of my favorite books on the famous prime minister is *Dinner with Churchill: Policy-Making at the Dinner Table* by Cita Stelzer. In it, I learned that Mr. Churchill had strong opinions about dining and always insisted on a round table with armchairs for himself and his fellow diners. Having visited Churchill's home, Chartwell, I remembered the round table surrounded by armchairs.

Coincidentally, a few months after devouring Stelzer's book, I was asked to design a show house room based on a favorite person in history in the cathedral at The Cathedral Antiques Show in Atlanta. Of course, Churchill immediately came to mind, and I was truly inspired by Stelzer's delightful and delicious tribute to Churchill's eating, drinking, and politicking! I can only imagine that an evening of dining with Churchill must have been one of the most memorable and enjoyable occasions for anyone lucky enough to have experienced it.

While in the process of designing this room, I had the honor of meeting the prime minister's great-grandson, Duncan Sandys, along with his beautiful wife and son, who live in Atlanta. I learned so much about Mr. Churchill and the family from Duncan, and he generously loaned me a portrait of my hero to hang in the room I designed.

Duncan also gave me a picture of the original dining room, which was a reminder of the wonderful memory of my visit to that room.

"My idea of a good dinner is to discuss good food, and, after this good food has been discussed, to discuss a good topic—with myself the chief conversationalist."

—WINSTON CHURCHILL

Never, never, never give up.

One of my favorite aspects of Mr. Churchill's personality was his wit and wisdom! For Churchill, dining was about not only good food, fine French champagne, and a good Havana cigar. He artfully used dining to display his conversational talents and to exert his power of persuasion—even with guests such as Franklin Roosevelt and Joseph Stalin, whom he attempted to persuade to fight WWII according to his strategic vision. In essence, the "British Bulldog" used dining and the dinner table to accomplish what often could not be accomplished at the conference table.

I read a great deal of WWII history, and most of these accounts center on Winston Churchill and the crucial role he played in the victory of England and the Allies. His determination and grit appeal to my personality, and his motto suits my life: "Never, never, never give up."

"Success is the ability to go from one failure to another with no loss of enthusiasm."

—WINSTON CHURCHILL

I knew Churchill had painted—often in his darkest moments—but I did not grasp the depth of his art until Duncan invited me to an exhibit of the leader's paintings he assembled for a show in Atlanta. Churchill's work, particularly his colors, fascinated me. Churchill started painting at the age of forty, shortly after the failed Dardanelles campaign that forced his resignation in 1915.

Overcome with what he referred to as "the black dog" of depression and anxiety, he was encouraged to paint by his sister-in-law, Lady Gwendoline Bertie. He was modest about his painting skills and insisted he was only a practicing amateur, but he was a prolific painter in the latter part of his life, creating over 550 works of art— all the while continuing to excel in writing and politics.

Churchill painted mostly impressionist landscapes using oils, but it's no surprise that I personally love his paintings of interiors. He was influenced by many of the top

It's a Birthday Blitz!

PLEASE JOIN WELLS AND KATHY
FOR COCKTAILS AND DINNER
TO CELEBRATE WINSTON CHURCHILL'S BIRTHDAY
AND SHARE OUR FAVORITE CHURCHILL BOOKS
TUESDAY 30 NOVEMBER
7:00 PM
CHATUGE COTTAGE

PLEASE RESPOND
KATHRYN@KATHRYNGREELEYDESIGNS.COM

Impressionist painters, such as Claude Monet and Paul Cézanne. In his book *Painting as a Pastime*, Churchill said this about color: "I cannot pretend to feel impartial about the colors; I rejoice with the brilliant ones and am genuinely sorry for the poor browns." After seeing the exhibit, I purchased several books of his paintings so I could study and savor them in my own little library.

Given his wit, determination, definite ideas on dining, appreciation for champagne, and his love of painting, it's no wonder that Winston Churchill is my favorite person in history. I believe our world today badly needs a Winston Churchill! Several of my friends share my fondness for Mr. Churchill, and like me, they read a great deal about him. I thought it would be lovely to create an opportunity to get together to drink some of Winston's favorite beverages, eat some of his favorite foods, and discuss our favorite Churchill books. So, what better way to celebrate my favorite person than a birthday celebration in his honor? Come with me on a little trip to Chatuge Cottage for a "Birthday Blitz" dinner that was the culmination of a long weekend house party on Churchill's birthday, November 30th. My small, square invitations were a heads-up to guests to bring their favorite book about Mr. Churchill.

My invitation included the famous profile of Churchill with his ever-present cigar. On an antique table in the keeping room, I created a small tableau of Mr. Churchill's distinct style including a cane, a bowler hat, a leather book on his wit and wisdom, a framed image of the dining room at Chartwell, and my bronze statue depicting him.

This casting is by Mark Gleason from Broken Stone Gallery. The inspiration for it came from a rare photograph of Churchill standing on a mound of rubble looking out on the early war ruins of London.

We started the evening in the keeping room with a cocktail of Churchill's favorite scotch, Johnnie Walker Black Label. For those non-scotch drinkers, we served Mr. Churchill's favorite champagne, Pol Roger. His love affair with Pol Roger is a thing of wine legends, and he is reputed to have drunk 42,000 bottles during his lifetime—and he only discovered it at age thirty-four! That equates to about two bottles per day. So, it is little wonder that this famous champagne house named its top cuvée in Churchill's honor. Needless to say, we had a good supply of Pol Roger for the evening!

As the sun dropped behind the mountains, leaving a soft glow on Lake Chatuge, we proceeded to the dining room for a meal of some of Mr. Churchill's favorite foods.

Table Inspiration

My collections often inspire my gatherings—and the design of my tabletops. My Jasperware collection began with a gift of a small cream-on-sage vase and grew from there. I have Royal Crown Derby's china pattern "Green Derby Panel" at Chestnut Cottage, and I use this pattern often. I decided to bring it to Chatuge Cottage for the Churchill dinner party to use alongside the celadon Jasperware. The dining table at Chatuge Cottage happens to be round, and six green leather armchairs surround it. I think Churchill would have most certainly approved of this!

I see nothing wrong with mixing a quintessential English pattern with a lovely French one.

I began the tabletop design with crisp white linen placemats and napkins, and then layered the "Green Derby Panel" with another china pattern—Bernardaud's "Constance."

I added salad-size accent plates in the "Green Derby Panel" pattern that have a beautiful floral motif.

As I wanted this to be a somewhat formal dinner party, I added sterling salts and peppers, my silver flatware pattern "Buttercup" by Gorham, and antique bone fish knives and forks. Sterling napkin rings in six different patterns held the linen napkins.

For this famous British gentleman, I thought it appropriate to use a Scottish stemware, "Thistle" by Edinburgh Crystal Company. But the celadon Jasperware collection was the real star of the table. I filled an urn with fresh white antique roses, and a variety of styles of small vases held the soft-apricot David Austin rose 'Juliet.' Eight Jasperware candlesticks with beeswax candles provided the perfect soft glow for the evening.

I selected the 'Juliet' roses as they reminded me of 'The Churchill Rose,' which is a shrub rose with lovely cupped, semi-double blooms in a unique shade of apricot. This rose was named in honor of the fiftieth anniversary of Churchill College, Cambridge, and chosen by Winston Churchill's youngest daughter, Lady Mary Soames. This rose was launched at the Chelsea Flower Show in 2011. After years of searching, I finally located a source for it (the British company Peter Beales Roses) and have just ordered one to add to the garden at Chestnut Cottage!

Mr. Churchill liked traditional English dishes like roast beef and Yorkshire pudding as much as he liked French cuisine. The first course of the evening was a filet of Dover sole wrapped in smoked salmon, followed by roast beef with Yorkshire pudding, English peas, and Pecorino-Garlic Duchess Potatoes. For dessert, I served an English trifle, which is a favorite of friends and family and something I often make during the holidays. We finished with a course of English cheeses and fresh pears since our "guest of honor" liked Stilton cheese more than sweet desserts (what the English generically refer to as "puddings"), but

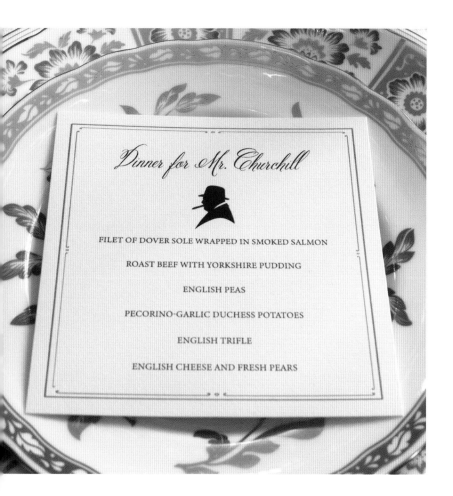

he was easily persuaded to have both when the opportunity arose. Hopefully, our menu would have pleased his palate!

Duchess Potatoes are French in origin, and not only do they instantly elevate the look of your dinner, I think they are the prettiest way to serve mashed potatoes! They are buttery on the inside, with crispy edges. Even though they look fancy, they are fairly simple to make. You'll find the recipe for these tasty potatoes in both French and American cookbooks. They just look so elegant on a silver serving tray, that they are well worth the bit of extra effort it takes to prepare them.

Mrs Grantham

Dinner for Mr. Churchill

FILET OF DOVER SOLE WRAPPED IN SMOKED SALMON

ROAST BEEF WITH YORKSHIRE PUDDING

ENGLISH PEAS

PECORINO-GARLIC DUCHESS POTATOES

ENGLISH TRIFLE

ENGLISH CHEESE AND FRESH PEARS

Mrs Anderson

Pecorino-Garlic Duchess Potatoes

INGREDIENTS

4 pounds Yukon Gold potatoes, peeled and cut into 1-inch cubes

2 tablespoons of salt, divided

4 tablespoons unsalted butter, cubed and softened (I measure using the lines on the butter wrapper)

¾ cup Pecorino Romano cheese, finely shredded

¼ cup heavy whipping cream, at room temperature

2 teaspoons garlic, minced

½ teaspoon fresh grated nutmeg

¾ teaspoon ground black pepper

6 egg yolks

4 tablespoons unsalted butter, melted

Chopped fresh chives and ground black pepper for garnish

PREPARATION

Preheat oven to 425 degrees. Line 2 rimmed, 9x13-inch baking sheets with parchment paper. Using a 3-inch round cutter, trace 24 circles, evenly spaced, on the 2 pieces of parchment.

In a large stockpot, cover the potatoes by 2 inches in cold water and add 1 tablespoon of salt. Bring to a boil over medium-high heat. Then reduce heat to medium-low and simmer until tender, about 15 minutes.

Drain the potatoes. Add softened butter, cheese, cream, garlic, pepper, nutmeg, and remaining 1 tablespoon of salt. Whip with an electric mixer until smooth. Let mix cool slightly and then stir in egg yolks and beat only until combined. Do not over-mix.

Transfer potato mixture to a large piping bag fitted with a ½-inch wide, open-star tip. I use an Ateco 827 piping tip.

Using the traced circles as guides, pipe potato mixture onto the prepared parchment paper. Then, using a silicone brush, gently brush the piped potato mixture with the melted butter. Bake until golden brown, about 20 minutes. Garnish with chives and pepper. Serve immediately.

An English trifle is a light "pudding" course, and it goes perfectly with a rather heavy meal of fish, roast beef and Yorkshire pudding, and Duchess Potatoes. I have made this recipe for years, and you can make it a day ahead. My version contains pound cake layered with vanilla custard, several fruits, and whipping cream. What else could anyone want? The custard is simple to make, delicious, and can be used in many different desserts—or just to feed your sweet grandchildren with a warm cookie!

I have never been proficient at making pound cakes. My mother made a delicious one, but I have just never mastered her recipe. On the other hand, I believe that if you can buy something better than what you can make, purchasing is the advisable route! Lucky for me, Cakes by Jane is in nearby Asheville. I send their pound cakes as gifts to friends and clients, and I pop into their wonderful, delicious-smelling little building whenever I am ready to make my trifle. They make a variety of flavors, but my favorite—particularly for this trifle—is almond.

The Wicked Wit of
Winston Churchill

Dominique Enright

English Trifle

INGREDIENTS

For the Vanilla Cream Custard

½ cup granulated sugar

¼ cup cornstarch

¼ teaspoon salt

2 cups whole milk

4 egg yolks, lightly beaten

1 teaspoon vanilla

For the Trifle

1 vanilla or almond pound cake

1 recipe of Vanilla Cream Custard

¼ cup cream sherry

6 kiwi fruits, peeled and thickly sliced crosswise

1 pint each of strawberries, blueberries, and
    raspberries

½ cup strawberry preserves

1½ cups of heavy cream, chilled

2 tablespoons confectioner's sugar

1 teaspoon of vanilla

Fresh mint

PREPARATION

The Vanilla Cream Custard

Combine the sugar, cornstarch, and salt in a heavy-bottom saucepan. With a whisk, stir in the milk and egg yolks. Place the mixture over medium heat, continuing to stir with the whisk to prevent scorching. When mixture comes to a low boil, remove from the heat. Stir in the vanilla. Cool. Place a piece of Press 'n Seal over the custard and place in refrigerator until set.

ASSEMBLING THE TRIFLE

Trim the crust off the pound cake and either enjoy or discard. Cut the cake into 1-inch cubes. Line the bottom of a trifle bowl with a layer of pound cake cubes, using about one-third of the cubes. Then sprinkle the cream sherry over the cake cubes. Place a layer of the custard over the center of the cubes, leaving the edges open. Place a layer of blueberries and then a layer of the raspberries in the space at the open edge of the bowl. Add another layer of the cake cubes and a layer of the custard, again leaving the edges open. This time, line the space at the outside wall of the bowl with slices of kiwi fruit, displaying the cross sections of the fruit. Layer the remaining kiwi fruit on top of the custard. Add the final layer of cake cubes and custard, extending them to the edge of the bowl. Add a layer of the strawberry preserves. Follow with a layer of raspberries around the edge of the bowl and blueberries in the center. Just before serving, whip the cream with the sugar and vanilla. Top the trifle with the whipped cream and garnish with whole strawberries, strawberry halves, blueberries, and a sprig or two of fresh mint.

I used an antique English oak sideboard in my dining room to serve several of the menu courses. I brought out more Jasperware, including a large vase filled with white antique roses and a very heavy cheese dome to hold a variety of English cheeses for the final course.

I'm sure that Mr. Churchill enjoyed celebrating each and every one of his birthdays, and I did chuckle at what he said on his seventy-fifth birthday on November 30, 1949:

"I am ready to meet my Maker. Whether my Maker is prepared for the great ordeal of meeting me is another matter."

After dinner, we gathered back in the keeping room by the fire with more scotch and champagne to discuss our favorite books about the man of the hour. As guests left the following morning, everyone was given their own copy of *The Wicked Wit of Winston Churchill*.

Every time I read this book of Churchill quotes, I find myself laughing out loud, so hopefully these favors will provide guests a few good laughs as well. What a lovely end to an autumn weekend house party! I will leave you with one last quote, which truly sums up who this great man really was and what he meant to history.

"We shall go on to the end, we shall fight in France, we shall fight on the seas and oceans, we shall fight . . . in the air, we shall defend our Island, whatever the cost may be, we shall fight on the landing grounds, we shall fight in the fields and in the streets, we shall fight in the hills; we shall never surrender . . ."

—WINSTON CHURCHILL, in a speech following the evacuation of the British Expeditionary Force from Dunkirk (JUNE 4, 1940)

Collecting

Barley Twist and Wedgwood Jasperware

I deeply love all of my collections at the cottage. However, my affection for the barley twist candlesticks has been the longest and most enduring. I have been adding to it for many years. As you may have noticed, the design is all around the cottage—in most every room, on candlesticks, and on antique furniture. I treasured my first pair of these candlesticks and began to be obsessed with finding more. When I wanted lots of candlelight for the Tuscan dinner, they were the perfect collection for that special table.

The words "barley twist" always sound like an old-fashioned soda or confection. In fact, an older, and much less used variation is "barley-sugar twist." Barley-sugar twist candy was a treat popular in the 1600s originally made from hot sugar syrup with an extract of barley to color it. This particular shape dates back hundreds of years, stemming from the architectural "Solomonic column," a decoration found in the architecture of ancient Greek and Roman civilizations. The "Solomon" in the term comes from the belief that helix-shaped columns were used as structural pillars for the roof of Solomon's Temple in the Bible. You will still find Solomonic columns in architecture today and also in a vast assortment of decorative applications. I have even noticed this design in fabrics!

I am totally intrigued by the precision of the hand-carved barley twist candlesticks, but my interest doesn't stop there. Early barley twist furniture was also created by hand, and I so admire the meticulous measuring skills that must have gone into making the curves so exact and evenly spaced. Think of the planning and patience it took to get the design right before the carving could even begin. Eventually a technique was developed to turn pieces of wood on a lathe, and the curves were carved as the wood turned on this mechanism. In the late seventeenth century, the spiral form became a popular feature in furniture, particularly as legs and column decorations in English, French, and Dutch pieces. The twists were most commonly carved from oak, but fine examples exist also in walnut.

A variation of barley twist is called *open* barley twist, with "open" meaning hollow. In antique furniture, this open twist design was rather uncommon, because it took away from the strength that gave the column structural integrity. This design was most often found in smaller items, such as candlesticks. I prize my open twist candlesticks and am always on the hunt for this style! As you look around Chestnut Cottage, you will find the barley twist design in both new and antique pieces.

A few years ago, I used barley twist balustrades in designing a staircase for one of my design projects. I fell in love with the staircase and decided to do the same when I recently re-designed Chatuge Cottage! I think this design creates instant Old World charm.

You will find this detail repeated in most every room of Chatuge Cottage.

In the dining room . . .

In the kitchen . . .

In the upstairs guest suite . . .

Particularly on this Scottish chest . . .

This chest is one of my favorite pieces of furniture and is a perfect fit for a Scottish-themed guest bedroom.

On the upstairs landing . . .

Barley twist in every nook and cranny!

One could safely say that this antique design detail is one of my favorites!

Another little collection that you might notice at Chatuge Cottage is my black cabinet filled with red transferware. Before making the carport into the dining room at this cottage, I had a collection of red transferware in the pre-renovation kitchen. I just couldn't bear to get rid of this collection, so I picked my favorite pieces and now enjoy them in the dining room, combined with my blue transferware.

Collecting Wedgwood Jasperware is a fairly recent passion. I love all sorts of shapes and sizes. As I mentioned earlier, when a friend gave me a small sage-green Jasperware vase as a hostess gift, I could not resist acquiring more and more pieces. Wells knew an antique dealer friend and put him on the hunt. On a recent Christmas morning, I found two boxes of beautiful sage Jasperware under our tree. One box from Wells and another from my close friend Holli Morris!

This collection even inspired the design of our master bedroom at Chatuge Cottage. After studying the soft green-with-cream color combination, I instantly knew the fabric that had to go with this collection: Colefax and Fowler's "Bowood." This classic fabric design is based on a document originally discovered by John Beresford Fowler at Bowood House in England. Fowler was a designer who became known as the master of the English Country look. He was taken with how the fabric allowed "the garden to spill into the rooms." Its greens, grays, and warm cream background made it a perfect companion to the sage Jasperware! I love this fabric so much that I upholstered all the walls, two chairs, a headboard, a dust ruffle, and two decorative pillows with it. It is definitely a "Bowood" room!

Tabletops are filled with the sage Jasperware, the antique secretary is filled with Jasperware, and so is even the top of a little faux bamboo bookcase.

Jasperware pottery was first developed by Josiah Wedgwood in the 1770s. It is often referred to as stoneware and has an unglazed matte "biscuit" finish. While the exact Wedgwood formula remains confidential, analyses indicate that barium sulphate is a key ingredient.

Jasperware was produced in over thirty different colors, ranging from vibrant crimson and sage to royal blue, yellow, and even black, and some rare tri-colored pieces. The most common and popular color is a pale blue that has become known as Wedgwood Blue. Among the various shades of green that the Wedgwood factory produced, it is the lighter variety, sage, that attracted the most attention and is seen most often.

Duncan MacDuff even enjoys sitting surrounded by "Bowood" and Jasperware.

A first viewing of Wedgwood Jasperware typically elicits a reaction of awe due to its delicate elegance. Relief decorations in contrasting colors, typically white, in classical motifs were produced in molds and applied to the ware as sprigs. Later, Wedgwood turned to leading artists outside the usual world of Staffordshire pottery for designs. High-quality portraits, mostly in profile, were added to the gallery of options. Jasperware has been made into a great variety of decorative objects but was not typically used for tableware or tea ware, even though you can find a few serving pieces.

Wedgwood Jasperware can often be dated by the style of potter's marks. Before 1860, the mark reads "Wedgwood" and is usually accompanied by other potter markings and a single letter. From 1860 to 1929, you'll see a three-letter mark representing, in order, the month, the potter, and the year. The year code starts mid-alphabet with the letter "O" for 1860, the letter "P" for 1861, etc., returning to "A" after "Z." For certain letters, there are two possible year dates. Unfortunately, these date codes were used infrequently on Jasperware pieces. A single letter is more commonly found during this time period, but it is merely a potter's mark and unhelpful in dating the object. From 1891 to 1908, the marks say "Wedgwood" and "England" and are most commonly separated. From 1908 to 1969, the marks read "Wedgwood" and "Made in England." After 1929, the typeface of the word "Wedgwood" was changed to sans serif. From 1970 to the present, the mark is "Wedgwood Made in England" as a single stamp.

Simple Pleasures

CELEBRATING AUTUMN:
APPLES, DAHLIAS, AND PUMPKINS, OH MY!

*"Autumn is the mellower season, and what we lose
in flowers we more than gain in fruits."*

—SAMUEL BUTLER

Autumn is a time of many simple pleasures at Chestnut Cottage. But I'll only mention three here. We have many apple orchards in our area, so the fruit is plentiful. For my Dreaming of Tuscany dinner, I made my Apple Tart. Another favorite at Chestnut Cottage is a Fresh Apple Cake. This cake is already moist, but the glaze makes it extra moist! I usually make it in a sheet pan if I am taking it to someone else, but if I am serving this cake at home, the Bundt pan makes a very nice presentation. Either way, this cake just says autumn to me.

Fresh Apple Cake

INGREDIENTS

For the Cake

3 cups Red Delicious apples, peeled and cut into ¼-inch cubes

1 teaspoon salt

1 teaspoon baking soda

2 cups granulated sugar

3 eggs

1½ cups canola oil

1½ teaspoon pure vanilla extract

3 cups all-purpose flour

1 cup pecans, coarsely chopped

1 cup shredded coconut, thawed if previously frozen

For the Glaze

1 cup brown sugar

1 stick unsalted butter

¼ cup whole milk

PREPARATION

Preheat oven to 325 degrees. Sprinkle the soda and salt over the cubed apples. In a separate bowl, combine sugar, oil, and eggs, and then stir in flour, vanilla, apples, pecans, and coconut. Mix well by hand. Batter will be thick. Spray a Bundt, tube, or sheet pan with Baker's Joy or other cooking spray. Pour the batter into the pan and bake for 1 hour and 20 minutes. Take pan out of oven, cool for 10 minutes, and unmold onto a wire rack. Prick the top of the cake with a toothpick.

For the glaze, in a heavy-bottom saucepan, heat sugar, butter, and milk to a low boil, and cook for 2½ minutes. Move the cake to your serving plate. Using a silicone brush, spread the glaze carefully over the warm cake, avoiding run-off.

I always enjoy making the cottage festive in the days leading up to our big Thanksgiving meal. You may remember our Thanksgiving gathering in *The Collected Tabletop*. I particularly like white pumpkins, as they make a nice, neutral vessel for an autumn cut-flower arrangement. The garden keeps giving dahlias, a few stems of monk's hood, a bit of safflower, the delicate little gaillardia, and a variety of lovely ferns. A friend keeps me supplied with beautiful red zinnias to add to this mix.

During the autumn season, the library mantel always gets decorated with bittersweet and my little collection of David Goldhagen art glass cobalt pumpkins, along with the work of another glass blower, Kenny Piper. The vase he created is one for all seasons, and in autumn, the orange dahlias are a beautiful contrast with the cobalt art glass pieces.

There are so many autumn simple pleasures to delight in, but now I must be thinking ahead to the Christmas season at Chestnut Cottage! With seven live trees to decorate, it's time to leave the joys of autumn behind until next year.

Winter

"Winter is the time for comfort, for good food and warmth, for the touch of a friendly hand and for a talk beside the fire: it is the time for home."

—EDITH SITWELL

Buried Treasure

In dreary winter who would know
My garden's hidden loveliness?
Though Spring will banish frost and snow,
In dreary winter who would know
That here my crocuses will grow,
And fill my eyes with happiness.
In dreary winter who would know
My garden's hidden loveliness?

—ELIZABETH BARRETT
FROM *MY GARDEN*

In the Garden

By winter's eve, the garden at Chestnut Cottage has been lovingly put to bed for a long winter's nap. However, that doesn't mean the excitement has stopped. This is a very busy time of year at the cottage. Depending on the weather, there are spring bulbs to plant, and as soon as the garden is put to bed, I'm already plotting and planning next year's garden on my sketchpad indoors!

A few early, beautiful Helleborus niger 'Jacob' light up the beds with their brilliance.

There are window boxes and containers to fill with fresh holiday greens and our own scarlet winterberries—assuming the birds haven't feasted on all the berries! I always feel a bit sad when the summer window boxes are finished, but knowing I will fill them again for the Christmas season makes me happy.

Decorating the garden and exterior of your home should be as natural as decorating the interior during this special season. A little attention to the exterior details will make sure you offer a very warm holiday welcome.

I always source my wreaths for the gate and the front door from our local farmer's market and add my own plaid bows!

Any amount of snow we get at Chestnut Cottage brings me great joy, and a light snow in January just after New Year's was the beginning of more to come!

A snowstorm in late January yielded more than a foot of snow on the Chestnut Garden.

Even a foot of snow did not keep the Edgeworthia bush, commonly known as the paper bush, from putting out its blossoms.

The snow brought thick cushions to the teak garden furniture.

I always think a blanket of snow makes the winter garden look so sculptural.

The garden looks quiet and restful, but a flurry of activity has taken over inside the house.

I patiently wait for more of the hellebores to make their showing as I dream of the spring garden!

Shall we go inside where the heavenly smell of beautiful, fresh evergreens and holiday baking greets us at the cottage door?

Decking the Halls

Christmas is a reminder that the garden provides us with beauty year-round. As you know from the other chapters in this book, I wholeheartedly believe in bringing this beauty indoors. The smell of fresh trees and greens throughout the season is a special joy, and for me, it far outweighs the conveniences of artificial versions. This time of year, the garden provides greens of pine, holly, ivy, boxwood, and winterberry for the cottage's Christmas display, and I also source greens from local growers. I always make a boxwood tree a year for the kitchen from the oldest and largest boxwood in the garden.

One of my neighbors graciously lets me gather magnolia from his yard to round out my Christmas decorating greens.

The leftovers from our annual Thanksgiving meal for family and friends are barely put away when it's time to breathe the spirit of Christmas into all the rooms in the cottage.

This season is my very favorite time of the year, and memories of my childhood Christmases warm my heart and fuel my passion for the holiday.

Each year, I am amazed Wells has not divorced me for insisting that we put up seven fresh trees! But he continues to indulge my passion, and I do believe he enjoys them just as much as I do. Our favorite local Christmas tree farm, Boyd's Tree Farm, is nationally known. Our friend Amy Spivey, who works at the farm, selects all seven trees, brings them to the cottage, and helps us get them into their stands. What a blessing she has been over the years!

Of course, to properly decorate these seven trees, I must climb up into the attic and bring down my wonderful collection of ornaments. I keep each tree's decorations separate so I can take the specific ornaments directly to the room where that tree will be trimmed. Once they're finished, I know they will bring so much joy to everyone who visits the cottage.

I love the classic combination of red and green. However, I always mix in some gold for a more festive mood! And I add a bit of pattern with plaids and tartans on my gift wrap, stockings, and other accent pieces. There's much to be done, so I start early on painting our Christmas card—which always includes Duncan MacDuff.

There are invitations to get out for our holiday gatherings.

And there are windows to fill with greens and candles, mantels to decorate, and containers to fill.

I love filling my antique Flow Blue punch bowl with orchids, pine, winterberries, and magnolia to display on the piano. And I bring in a boxwood ball topiary from the garden to display in a blue and white fishbowl.

During the holidays, a very special plaid bear sits in our keeping room. Margaret Bear, named after my mother, always sits in this particular antique chair because my mother loved to sit in it when we opened gifts on Christmas morning.

For me, Christmas is steeped in ritual and tradition.

When my mother passed away, I gave several items of her clothing to a friend, Mickie Norman. Mickie gave a plaid Pendleton jacket with black velvet buttons and ribbon to her aunt Patsy, who lovingly took the jacket apart and made this very precious little bear for me. Her eyes are made from the velvet buttons, which also accent her front. Patsy even took the Pendleton tag from inside the jacket and made it into a pocket on the bear's backside. Margaret Bear keeps company with holiday images of my two favorite Westies and a naughty girl trying to convince Santa that she had indeed been a good girl!

But the real reason for the season is on display with my Waterford nativity set, which was given to me by my mother-in-law, piece by piece, each year at Christmas, until the set was complete.

The old chestnut mantel in the library overflows with greens and candles and the stockings are hung by two chimneys with care!

The little bamboo vase that I keep in the library is truly a vase for all seasons.

So many trees to decorate and so many ornaments to unpack . . . but we will get to that a bit later!

When I look around the cottage, I have to say it is truly "the most wonderful time of the year"!

Gatherings

Christmas Ornament
Brunch for the Bride

Christmas Ornament Brunch for the Bride Menu

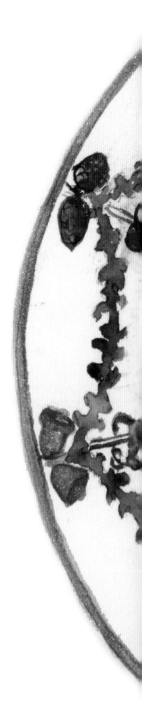

Christmas Cosmopolitans

Individual Quiche Lorraine with Cucumber-Boursin Rollups

Night-Before French Toast

Fresh Fruit Kabobs

Sausage Muffins and Cheddar Scones

Sour Cream Coffee Cake and Pecan Snowballs

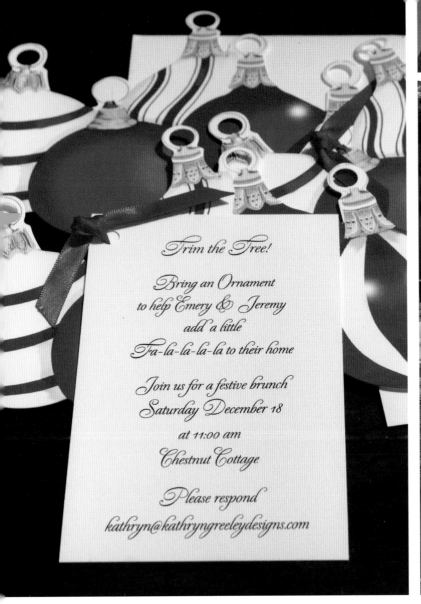

One of my favorite things to do for a new bride is to give an ornament shower to trim her first tree. So many young brides start their married life with nothing for their first tree, and ornaments can be expensive for a couple, especially at Christmastime.

My young friend Emery Morris was married in October, so an early-December ornament shower brunch seemed a perfect way to start the holiday entertaining. The themed invitation asks guests to bring an ornament for the tree that she and her husband, Jeremy, will decorate in their home. I also encouraged our guests to bring lights, garlands, or other tree-trimming items they thought the bride and groom might enjoy.

A group of twelve friends made a nice gathering, with six seated around each of our two round tables.

Window boxes and planters full of Christmas greens and berries greeted guests as they entered at the kitchen door.

Table Inspiration

My table designs began with Brunschwig and Fils's "Wood Leaf" faux bois fabric in both green and red that I had made into tablecloths to fit sixty-inch round tables. To create a casual "woodsy" scheme, I used my collection of Simon Pearce trees.

These lovely glass trees are American made, from Vermont, and my collection includes their classic Vermont Evergreens and a few of their Bubble Evergreens. They make a lovely centerpiece when surrounded with holly, pine, arborvitae, ivy, winterberries, and magnolia from the garden. I also added a few red 'Freedom' roses to punch up the holiday color scheme. Candles add a soft glow to the table, even early in the day.

The tables included a mix of Royal Copenhagen's "Star Fluted" china alongside Herend's "Princess Victoria" in dark green. "Star Fluted," which is made in Denmark, has a garland of spruce that winds its way through bows, hearts, drums, and angels—the staples of a traditional, cozy Danish Christmas. It's fun to note that no two bows on this pattern are exactly the same!

The "Princess Victoria" pattern is a perfect pairing with its simplistic yet stunning dark-green border that has intricate white detailing. Made in Hungary, this pattern also works wonderfully in its own right for those who are looking for an understated, elegant look. Because I wanted the whites of the patterns to be consistent, I found Royal Copenhagen's "Full Lace" matched perfectly for the bread-and-butter plates.

For the table with the green faux bois cloth, "Twisted Soraya" Murano stemware made by Nason Moretti added a crisp pop of color.

I dearly love this stemware pattern, and only wish I could also have it in blue. There's just simply no more room at the cottage for yet another stemware pattern! I used Waterford "Lismore," including the "Twelve Days of Christmas" champagne flutes in this pattern.

I really enjoy brunch gatherings. Perhaps that is because I love to prepare and eat almost anything on a brunch menu!

I served several of my favorite brunch items—Mini Sausage Muffins, Sour Cream Coffee Cake, Night-Before French Toast, and my mother's special Pecan Snowballs. Never a Christmas will pass that I don't make these yummy Snowballs!

But first things first!

We started our festivities with Christmas Cosmopolitans.

While sipping these tasty cocktails, Emery opened her "Bride's Box." I had been collecting ornaments for several months that reflected Emery's and Jeremy's interests.

Emery loves cooking and Jeremy is a contractor who loves golf and fishing. Two dogs are a part of their little family, so I included a dog bone for their tree. I couldn't resist the Santa with the mask because Emery and Jeremy had been forced to delay their wedding for many months due to the pandemic. Emery and my husband both love puzzles, so Wells contributed a Christmas ornament puzzle for her as well. My little boxwood tree held ornament frames with pictures of the couple's wedding day. These were given as favors to each guest.

I customarily do my Night-Before French Toast as a casserole, but for this brunch I used a tree-shaped cookie cutter to cut the casserole into tree shapes, which works nicely if you use Brioche bread. Often, I top the casserole with blueberries and maple syrup, but since I was serving Fresh Fruit Kabobs, I offered maple syrup on the side.

Night-Before French Toast

INGREDIENTS

1 long, thin French baguette
  (about 10 ounces) or a loaf of Brioche
  bread, about 18 inches long

8 large eggs

3 cups whole milk

¼ cup sugar

¾ teaspoon salt

1 tablespoon pure vanilla extract

2 tablespoons unsalted butter

Ground cinnamon to sprinkle

Maple syrup and blueberries for
  finishing (optional)

PREPARATION

Grease a 13x9-inch baking dish.

Cut the bread into 18 slices (approximately ¾-inch wide). Arrange the slices in one layer in the bottom of the greased dish. Beat eggs, milk, sugar, salt, and vanilla together in a large mixing bowl. When thoroughly blended, pour mixture over the bread. The bread will float to the top of the pan.

Cut the butter into about 20 small pieces. Dot each piece of bread with one piece of butter and sprinkle cinnamon lightly over the whole dish. Cover. Refrigerate overnight or up to 36 hours to allow the bread to absorb the liquid.

When ready to bake, preheat oven to 350 degrees. Uncover and bake for 45 minutes or until puffy and light brown. Remove from the oven and allow to set for 5 minutes.

Serve with warm maple syrup and fresh blueberries as desired.

Many years ago, my friend Annette gave me the recipe for her very moist and delicious Sour Cream Coffee Cake, and I always use this wreath pan I found at Williams-Sonoma during the holiday season. I like to keep one of these coffee cakes in the freezer at Chestnut Cottage to pull out for overnight guests or for a quick, homemade hostess gift. At the ornament shower, we finished our brunch with this cake and Pecan Snowballs.

Sour Cream Coffee Cake

INGREDIENTS

For the Cake

2 sticks unsalted butter, softened

2 cups granulated sugar, sifted

2 large eggs

1 cup sour cream

1 teaspoon pure vanilla extract

2 cups Swann's Down cake flour, sifted
   (or your favorite brand)

1 teaspoon salt, sifted

1 teaspoon baking powder, sifted

For the Topping

6 tablespoons brown sugar

2½ teaspoons ground cinnamon

1 cup chopped pecans

PREPARATION

Preheat oven to 350 degrees and grease and flour a 10-inch tube or Bundt pan. Blend together by hand the softened butter, eggs, sugar, sour cream, and vanilla extract. Sift the cake flour, salt, and baking powder together and add to the egg and butter mixture. For the topping, mix sugar, cinnamon, and pecans together.

Pour half of the batter into the pan. Sprinkle half of the topping over the batter. Add the remaining batter and then top with the remaining topping mix. Bake for 40-45 minutes. Remove from oven and let the cake set in the pan for about 5 minutes. Then turn out onto a wire cooling rack and cool completely.

Pecan Snowballs

INGREDIENTS

2 cups unsalted butter, at room
temperature

1 cup confectioner's sugar

2 teaspoons pure vanilla extract

½ teaspoon salt

4 cups White Lily all-purpose flour
(or your favorite brand)

2 cups chopped pecans

1 pound of confectioner's sugar
for coating

PREPARATION

Preheat oven to 350 degrees and line a cookie sheet with parchment or a silicone baking mat.

In a stand mixer fitted with a paddle attachment, cream the butter and sugar together. This can also be done in a large bowl with a hand mixer. Add the vanilla and salt and mix well. Slowly add the flour, mixing well. A thick dough will form.

Add the chopped pecans and mix well. Cover and refrigerate for 30 minutes.

Remove from refrigerator and scoop dough by tablespoons and roll into 1-inch balls (about the size of a large marble). The dough may seem crumbly but continue to roll in the palm of your hand until the dough forms a ball.

Place balls on prepared baking sheet about 2 inches apart. Bake for 12–15 minutes until slightly brown. Remove from the oven and let cool slightly. While the snowballs are still warm, roll in the confectioner's sugar. Let cool completely and then roll in confectioner's sugar two more times.

Makes about 60 snowballs.

A final addition to the brunch menu were my Mini Sausage Muffins. In *The Collected Tabletop*, I shared my recipe for cheddar scones, but another easy brunch or breakfast treat are these muffins, which I also try to keep a supply of in my freezer. They bring a savory flavor to pair with the many sweet treats we often enjoy during brunch.

Mini Sausage Muffins

INGREDIENTS

1 pound country or breakfast sausage, cooked and drained well (do not use spicy sausage)

1 10.5-ounce can of cheddar cheese soup

½ cup whole milk

1 cup grated sharp cheddar cheese

1 teaspoon hot sauce (like Tabasco)

3 cups Bisquick pancake mix

PREPARATION

Preheat oven to 400 degrees and grease a mini muffin pan. Mix the cooked sausage, soup, milk, cheese, and hot sauce together in a large bowl. Gradually stir in the Bisquick. The dough will be very sticky. Spoon into mini muffin pan and bake for about 15 minutes, until golden brown.

Makes about 24 mini muffins.

Note: If I plan to freeze these muffins, I only bake them for about 10 minutes, let them cool on a cooling rack, then place them in freezer bags. Upon removing the muffins from the freezer when you are ready to use, bake an additional 5–7 minutes.

'Twas the Night
Before Christmas

'Twas the Night Before Christmas

Menu

Prawn Cocktail in Martini Glasses

Arugula Salad with Goat Cheese and Cranberries

Beef Wellington

Scalloped Potatoes

Asparagus Bundles

Pinch Bread

Bûche de Noël

It has become a tradition at Chestnut Cottage to have family and friends over for cocktails and dinner on Christmas Eve. By now, the trees are all up, the greens are hung, the mantels are ready, there's a nice fire roaring, and it's time to relax and savor the true meaning of this joyous season.

A gate-fold card invited special friends and family to join us for this special evening.

Wells is always our bartender, and he loves using our Kenny Pieper martini glasses. Years ago, I commissioned Kenny to make a collection of twelve red and gold martini glasses for a client, and then I decided I must have some for myself! Kenny is an internationally recognized and exhibited glassblower who has been perfecting his craft since his days as a teenager studying at the Penland School of Crafts here in the Blue Ridge Mountains. The details within each glass are intricate and minute, and no two of the twelve are alike. On Christmas Eve, these lovely glasses have a dual purpose, serving beverages at the bar and then holding our prawn cocktail at dinner.

Our "Night on the Town Fairy" quietly watches over the bar activities!

Table Inspiration

Like other traditions at Chestnut Cottage, my Christmas Eve table design rarely changes. I use all my favorite holiday patterns, most of which I have had for decades. Some time ago, I purchased sixteen delightful holly placemats at Quintessentials in Raleigh. Dinner plates rest snugly on these textured mats, and they work with almost any holiday china pattern. Too bad I didn't buy hundreds, because they are no longer available and everyone who sees them falls in love with them.

My two favorite holiday china patterns are "Holly Ribbons" by Royal Worcester and "Christmas Rose" by Spode. "Holly Ribbons" features gold trim with iridescent holly berries and red ribbons entwined with holly leaves and mistletoe. Spode's "Christmas Rose" is an elegant pattern as stylish today as it was when it was first produced in 1890. The distinctive design includes a border of Lenten roses, holly leaves, and berries and mistletoe. Interestingly enough, this design was first featured on a plum pudding dish and proved so popular that a complete dinnerware service was created.

For this occasion, I set two tables—one in the kitchen and one in the keeping room. As I keep my Simon Pearce trees on the kitchen table throughout the holidays, they were the start of the table design for the kitchen table.

I love using the trees without a tablecloth so that the beauty of the wood table can be fully seen and appreciated. A casual red tartan napkin is perfect for this table.

I selected the same china and placemats for both tables, and a combination of stemware on the kitchen table included Saint Louis "Tommy" and William Yeoward "Fern."

With its pale green tablecloth and antique linen napkins, the table in the keeping room had a bit more of a formal feel. One of my favorite silver pieces, given to me by Wells one year for Christmas, holds greens, roses, and candles at the center of this table.

"Thistle" by Edinburgh Crystal is the stemware for this table, and I suppose if I had to choose only one crystal pattern as my favorite, this would be it. Both tables had a forest of David Goldhagen's colorful little blown glass trees holding place cards.

No Christmas Eve gathering would be complete without Christmas crackers! Christmas crackers are an English tradition dating back to Victorian times, when in the early 1850s, London confectioner Tom Smith started adding a sliver of paper containing a love message similar to that in a fortune cookie to his sugared almond bonbons that he sold in twisted paper packages. The story goes that when he heard the crackle and "bang" of a log he had just put on the fire, he decided to create a new log-shaped package that would produce a bang when it was pulled open at either end. In the early 1900s, his son Walter added paper crowns and trinkets to the packages, and the bonbons eventually gave way to little gifts and small papers printed with mottos, jokes, riddles, or charades. I always end our Christmas Eve gathering with Christmas crackers, as both young and old enjoy the bang, the trinkets, the riddles, and most of all, the paper crowns! We wear our crowns while we have another glass of champagne and wash all the dishes. It is rumored that the Queen even wears her paper crown at Christmas lunch!

We end our Christmas Eve gathering with a beautiful Bûche de Noël, also known as the Christmas Yule Log. After a rather long and heavy meal and lots of good wine, this is a light, refreshing dessert. I add chocolate toffee to my recipe and always enjoy making the Meringue Mushrooms to give it a very rustic look. It would not be Christmas without the Bûche de Noël.

I find the history of the Bûche de Noël fascinating. The tradition dates back to medieval times, a period when many pagan rites were competing with Christmas traditions. In France, a log of wood—often from a fruit tree to ensure a successful harvest in the year to come—would be brought home and placed on the hearth, the center of family activity. Depending on the region and its various beliefs, the log was blessed, decorated with ribbons and greenery, and then salt, wine, or holy water might be sprinkled on top of it before lighting it on the fire. For example, sprinkling wine was a way in which to guarantee the following year's grape harvest would be bountiful.

Once the log was lit on Christmas Eve, it had to burn for at least three days for good luck, but would, ideally, last until the New Year. Little by little, traditional hearths disappeared in homes, being replaced by wood-burning stoves for cooking. With no center stage left for the Christmas log ritual, smaller logs were placed as a decorative reminder on tabletops, and it was only a matter of time before someone realized it would be a lot nicer to eat the log rather than simply look at it. That's how the Bûche de Noël dessert was born!

The custom of the rolled cake dates back to the Victorian era, when it became fashionable to serve a thin sponge cake rolled with jam or cream filling and covered with buttercream. Flavors and types of filling varied by region, but the meringue mushrooms were most always included as a traditional decoration. Whatever style of cake is eaten, the Yule Log still does one thing: It brings family and friends together on Christmas!

Bûche de Noël

INGREDIENTS

For the Cake

4 large eggs, separated

⅔ cup granulated sugar

1 tablespoon pure vanilla extract

⅓ cup all-purpose flour

¼ cup unsweetened cocoa powder

¼ teaspoon salt

½ teaspoon baking powder

For the Filling

2 cups whipping cream

¼ cup confectioner's sugar

3 tablespoons Marshmallow Fluff

¾ cup of finely chopped toffee

1 teaspoon pure vanilla extract

For the Frosting

1 ½ cups unsalted butter, softened

1 cup unsweetened cocoa

5 cups confectioner's sugar

½ cup whole milk

2 teaspoons pure vanilla extract

For the Meringue Mushrooms

3 egg whites

¼ teaspoon cream of tartar

¼ teaspoon salt

¾ cup granulated sugar

6 ounces dark chocolate chips

Cocoa powder for dusting

PREPARATION

The Cake

Preheat oven to 375 degrees. Line a jelly roll pan (typically 10½ x 15½ inches) with parchment paper and generously grease the parchment with cooking spray.

Beat egg whites until stiff and then fold in the sugar gradually. In another bowl, beat the egg yolks lightly and add vanilla.

Gently fold the egg white mixture into the yolks.

Sift the dry ingredients together. Fold the dry ingredients into the egg mixture. Pour batter into prepared pan and spread into an even layer. Bake until the top springs back when lightly pressed, about 12 minutes.

Dust a clean, dampened kitchen towel with confectioner's sugar and invert the warm cake onto the towel. Peel off the parchment paper. Use the towel to tightly roll the cake into a log. Cool for 30 minutes.

The Filling

Melt the Marshmallow Fluff in the microwave at 5-second intervals until just melted. Stir gently until slightly cooled and thick and gooey. In the bowl of a stand mixer fitted with a whisk attachment (or you can use a hand mixer), beat the whipping cream until soft peaks form. Stir the Marshmallow Fluff into the whipped cream followed by the confectioner's sugar and vanilla extract. Beat on high speed until stiff peaks form. Add the chopped toffee to the whipped cream mixture.

The Frosting

In the bowl of a stand mixer fitted with a paddle attachment, cream butter and cocoa powder until well combined. Alternately add sugar and milk to cocoa mixture by adding 1 cup of sugar, followed by a tablespoon of milk, 1 cup of sugar, etc., until all the sugar and milk has been added. Add vanilla and beat at high speed for 1 minute.

The Meringue Mushrooms (decoration)

Preheat the oven to 200 degrees. Line a rimmed baking sheet with parchment paper. In the bowl of a stand mixer fitted with the whisk attachment, beat egg whites, cream of tartar, and salt at low speed until foamy. With the mixer on high speed, add the sugar in a slow, steady stream. Beat until stiff peaks form.

Place meringue in a large piping bag fitted with a ½-inch round tip. Holding the tip perpendicular to the parchment paper, pipe half of meringue as mushroom tops, ¾ to 1½-inches across. Use a wet finger to press down any points. With the remaining meringue, pipe stems by holding the bag straight perpendicular to the parchment, pulling the bag straight up, making cylinders about 2 inches tall. Bake until meringues look dry, about 1¼–1½ hours. Turn off oven, open door, and let set overnight.

When ready to assemble, using the sharp tip of a paring knife, cut a hole in the underside of each mushroom cap, just large enough to insert the tip of the base, by inserting the knife tip in the center and gently rotating. Melt the chocolate and pipe a small amount into the hole in the mushroom cap. Stick the base into the hole and leave until the chocolate sets up. Dust with cocoa powder.

ASSEMBLING THE YULE LOG

Unroll the cake and spread the filling to within 1 inch of the edge. Roll the cake back up with the filling inside, using the towel again to help create a tight roll. Place seam side down onto a baking sheet and refrigerate until well chilled, about 1 hour.

When ready to serve, remove the log from the refrigerator, cut a small slice off each end to get a nice straight end, and frost the cake with the chocolate buttercream. Using a fork, gently make textured lines to resemble tree bark.

Garnish the log with the meringue mushrooms and seasonal greenery.

Note: I usually make two logs and cut one or two pieces off the second log to place on the sides of the roll to resemble a branch. Cut the "branch pieces" on a diagonal angle and fit them snugly on the sides of the log before frosting.

Raise Your Glass
to the New Year!

Raise Your Glass to the New Year!

Please Join Wells and Kathy

For a Black Tie Dinner

and

Champagne Tasting

Friday, December 31st

7:00 pm

Chestnut Cottage

Raise Your Glass to the New Year

Menu

Gougères

Caviar Dip on Homemade Potato Chips

Crab and Corn Chowder with Grilled Shrimp

Roasted Cornish Hens with Garlic and Rosemary

Oven-Roasted Brussels Sprouts on Lemon Ricotta

Wild Rice Pilaf with Butternut Squash, Pecans, and Cranberries

Chocolate Mousse Cake

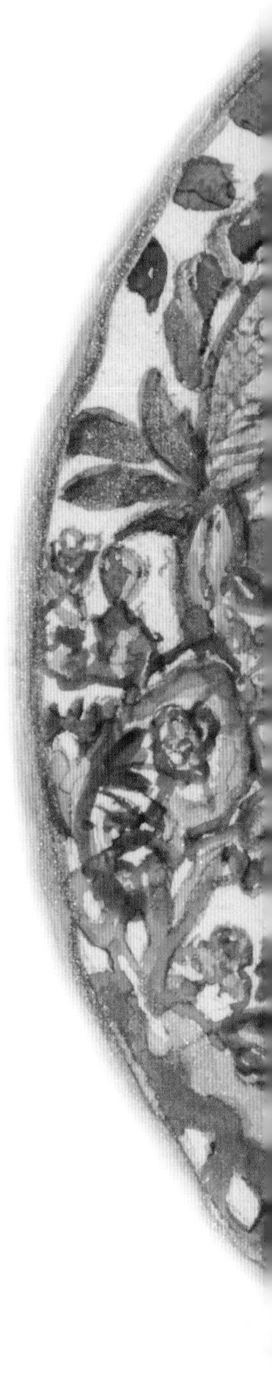

Wells and I much prefer a small dinner party with a few friends on New Year's Eve, rather than a big affair with a cast of hundreds. As my alcohol of choice is always champagne, a black-tie champagne tasting and dinner always suits us for ringing in the New Year. My favorite champagne houses are Dom Perignon, Veuve Clicquot, Tattinger, and Pol Roger, and together these seem to be a perfect combination for a "tasting."

A gold gate-fold invitation—sent to a small number of close friends—sets the tone for a festive, formal evening.

On a recent trip to Burgundy, our wine guide gave me her grandmother's recipe for *gougères*. I thought they would be a nice starter with the champagne. These delightful French-style, savory pastries are made of choux dough loaded with Gruyère cheese. I served them alongside some delicious caviar dip. I always use Ina Garten's recipe for this dip, and I serve it with thinly sliced potatoes that have been brushed with olive oil and sea salt and then baked.

New Years Eve Menu

Gougeres

Caviar Dip on Homemade Potato Chips

Crab and Corn Chowder with Grilled Shrimp

Roasted Cornish Hens with Garlic and Rosemary

Oven Roasted Brussels Sprouts on Lemon Ricotta

Wild Rice Pilaf with Butternut Squash,
Pecans and Cranberries

Chocolate Mousse Cake

Gougères

INGREDIENTS

1 cup water

8 tablespoons unsalted butter

¾ teaspoon kosher salt

⅛ teaspoon freshly grated nutmeg

1¼ cups all-purpose flour

4 large eggs

1½ cups grated Gruyère cheese

½ teaspoon freshly ground black pepper

1 large egg yolk

PREPARATION

Preheat oven to 400 degrees. Line 2 baking sheets with parchment. Bring butter, salt, nutmeg, and water to a boil in a medium saucepan, stirring until butter is melted. Remove from heat, add flour, and stir to combine. Cook mixture over medium heat, stirring vigorously with a wooden spoon, until mixture pulls away from sides of pan and forms a ball, about 2 minutes.

Continue to cook, stirring vigorously, until a dry film forms on bottom and sides of pan and dough is no longer sticky, about 2 minutes longer. Remove pan from heat and let dough cool slightly, about 2 minutes.

Mix in whole eggs one at a time, incorporating fully between the addition of each egg. Mix in cheese and pepper. Scrape dough into a piping bag fitted with a ½-inch round tip. Pipe 1-inch rounds about 2 inches apart on baking sheets.

Whisk egg yolk and 1 teaspoon of water in a small bowl. Brush each round with egg wash.

Bake gougères until puffed and golden and dry in the center (they should sound hollow when tapped), about 20–25 minutes. Serve warm. Makes approximately 24.

Table Inspiration

As you may have already noticed, I have a great affection for china patterns from Royal Crown Derby. Their "Gold Aves" pattern is the focal point for this table design, and it ties back in with the gold invitation.

The intricate design of "Gold Aves" is hand decorated in 22-karat gold and has the quality of timeless opulence. The pattern is adopted from an embroidery by painter Albert Gregory and is adorned with dramatic birds of paradise and peacocks. This original pattern has appeared on Royal Crown Derby's tableware since 1932. I combined this pattern with Herend's "Golden Edge" and Annieglass "Ruffle" charger/buffet plates.

I felt these chargers gave a bit of a contemporary spin to a more classic, traditional tabletop. Bayel Crystal's "Palais" glassware with its intricate cut pattern features gold laurels and dots with a gold rim.

Gold beaded placemats finished the gold and white design along with this exquisite crystal pattern, which Bayel discontinued in 1970.

I find it hard to resist Leontine Linens, especially their napkins. For this occasion, I opted for a metallic gold thread, which formed a stylized monogram that completed the New Year's Eve table design!

A vase of cut glass and ormolu held an arrangement of 'Casa Blanca' lilies, a combination of white and green roses, and variegated pittosporum. I added a bit of 'Green Giant' arborvitae from the garden.

When you have a garden, you have something to bring inside in every season! A collection of Waterford candleholders surrounded the flowers and provided a soft light for the last festive evening of the year.

The menu for the evening started with crab and corn chowder topped with grilled shrimp. Roasted Cornish hens with garlic and rosemary, oven-roasted Brussels sprouts on lemon ricotta, and wild rice pilaf with butternut squash, pecans, and cranberries rounded out the main course.

We served the main course with a bottle of white Burgundy (Meursault Les Narvaux 2017) from the cellar.

We ended the evening with more champagne and one of my favorite chocolate desserts, Chocolate Mousse Cake! I have been making this recipe for years and often forget just how festive an end it brings to a meal.

Chocolate Mousse Cake

INGREDIENTS

For the Cake

7 ounces semisweet chocolate

¼ pound unsalted butter

7 large eggs, separated

1 cup granulated sugar, divided

1 teaspoon pure vanilla extract

⅛ teaspoon cream of tartar

For the Whipped Cream Frosting

1 pint heavy whipping cream

½ cup confectioner's sugar

1 teaspoon pure vanilla extract

PREPARATION

The Cake

Preheat oven to 325 degrees. In a small saucepan, melt chocolate and butter over low heat. In a large bowl, beat egg yolks and ¾ cup sugar until very light and fluffy, about 5 minutes. Gradually beat in the warm chocolate mixture and vanilla. In another large bowl, beat the egg whites with the cream of tartar until soft peaks form. Add the remaining ¼ cup of sugar, 1 tablespoon at a time. Continue beating until stiff. Fold egg white mixture carefully into the chocolate mixture.

Pour ¾ of the batter into an ungreased 9x3-inch springform pan. Cover the remaining mousse batter and refrigerate. Bake for 35 minutes. Remove the cake from oven and let cool completely. The cake will drop as it cools.

The Whipped Cream Frosting

In a small bowl, beat whipping cream until soft peaks form. Add confectioner's sugar and vanilla. Beat until stiff. Set aside.

ASSEMBLING THE CAKE

Remove cooled cake from the springform pan. Stir the refrigerated mousse batter to soften slightly. Spread on top of the cooled cake. Refrigerate until firm. Spread the Whipped Cream Frosting over the top of the cake. Garnish with chocolate leaves if desired.

The Chocolate Leaves

I like to garnish the chocolate mousse cake with chocolate leaves. All you will need are some non-poisonous leaves such as camellias or roses (I use 8–10 camellia leaves from the garden) and 4 ounces of semisweet baking chocolate.

Wash and dry the leaves. Line a baking sheet with wax paper. Melt the chocolate in the top of a double boiler over hot water. With a table knife or a small spatula, spread the melted chocolate over the underside of the leaves. A thick coating of the chocolate is best so that it doesn't break when removed. Place the leaves chocolate side up on the lined baking sheet. Refrigerate until the chocolate is firm. To remove the leaf, carefully grasp the leaf's stem and pull gently. The chocolate and the leaf will separate.

A word to the wise: I always break a few of the chocolate leaves when pulling them off the camellia leaf, so I always make extra!

*As soon as one year ends, we must begin
to celebrate the one that lies ahead!*

Health, Wealth,
Prosperity and Luck!

PLEASE JOIN US

AT CHESNUT COTTAGE

FOR NEW YEAR'S DAY
LUNCH

AT 1:00
SATURDAY, JANUARY 1

Health, Wealth, Prosperity and Luck Luncheon

Health, Wealth, Prosperity and Luck Luncheon

Menu

Black-Eyed Peas and Collard Greens Soup

Skillet Cornbread

Carrot Cake

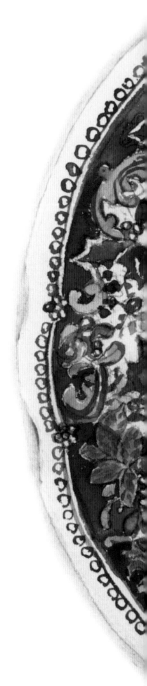

We Southerners love tradition, and New Year's Day is certainly no exception. So, we invited our guests from last night back for a special soup and lots of ball games!

Tradition states that the menu for lunch should symbolize health, wealth, prosperity, and luck. Who knows what might happen if we don't serve the right dishes!?

In keeping with tradition, four essential components made up our meal.

Black eyed peas to bring luck and prosperity.

Collard greens to bring wealth, paper money, and health.

Owning pigs was historically a symbol of prosperity, and as pigs root forward when foraging, they also represent positive forward motion.

Finally, since cornbread symbolizes gold, its addition is always part of a successful New Year's Day menu!

With these dishes on New Year's Day, we're sure to get started on the right foot! My mother was never keen on cooking a big New Year's Day meal, but she always made a delicious soup that included all these ingredients, which she paired with a big pan of cornbread baked in a cast-iron skillet.

I have continued this tradition—as it's a simple and delicious way to get all the lucky ingredients in one bowl.

Black-Eyed Peas and Collard Greens Soup

INGREDIENTS

2 tablespoons vegetable oil

1 14-ounce package of Hillshire Farm
    smoked pork sausage, sliced

1 cup yellow onion, chopped

1 cup carrots, peeled and sliced

½ cup celery, sliced crosswise into
    ¼-inch pieces

3 cloves garlic, minced

1 32-ounce carton low-sodium
    beef broth

1 28-ounce can diced tomatoes, with
    the liquid

1 pound collard greens, stemmed and
    roughly chopped

1½ cups frozen black-eyed peas

¼ teaspoon salt

¼ teaspoon ground black pepper

1 tablespoon fresh thyme leaves

PREPARATION

In a Dutch oven or soup pot, heat oil over medium heat. Add sausage slices, onion, carrots, and celery and cook for approximately 8 minutes or until vegetables are tender, stirring frequently. Add garlic and thyme, stirring to combine. Add beef broth and tomatoes. Bring to a boil, add chopped collards, and stir well to combine all ingredients. Reduce heat to medium and cook until greens are wilted. Add the black-eyed peas, salt, and pepper. Cover and simmer for 30 to 40 minutes. Garnish with thyme, if desired.

Table Inspiration

I continue to keep my Simon Pearce trees on the kitchen table throughout most of the winter. On New Year's Day, I brought in more 'Green Giant' arborvitae from the garden and nestled it among the trees. I added small glass vases that hold a place card, and I filled each of them with a simple white rose.

Each year on the day after Thanksgiving, I bring out my everyday Christmas pattern, Spode's "Winter's Eve Blue (Camilla Shape)," and use it until the end of March. I love the intricate winter scenes and the shades of blue with the border of holly, pine, and ivy—all of which can be found in the garden at Chestnut Cottage!

Finally, Abigail's "Blue and White Swirl" stemware added a bit of whimsy to the table.

This simple lunch of soup and cornbread ended with my favorite Blue Ribbon Carrot Cake. This cake is so moist, and it freezes very nicely. I baked the cake in a sheet pan and then cut individual servings with a 3-inch baking ring. I thought the little cakes were more festive and would discourage overeating! With full tummies of prosperity and luck, we retired to the keeping room for an afternoon of college football.

Blue Ribbon Carrot Cake

INGREDIENTS

For the Cake

2 cups all-purpose flour

2 teaspoons baking soda

2 teaspoons ground cinnamon

½ teaspoon salt

3 eggs

¾ cup vegetable oil

¾ cup buttermilk

2 cups granulated sugar

2 teaspoons pure vanilla extract

1 8-ounce can crushed pineapple, drained

2 cups carrots, peeled and grated

3½ ounces shredded coconut, thawed if
    previously frozen

1 cup chopped pecans

For the Buttermilk Glaze

1 cup sugar

½ teaspoon baking soda

½ cup buttermilk

½ pound unsalted butter

1 tablespoon corn syrup

1 teaspoon pure vanilla extract

For the Cream Cheese Frosting

¼ pound unsalted butter, at room
    temperature

1 8-ounce package cream cheese, at room
    temperature

1 teaspoon pure vanilla extract

2 cups confectioner's sugar, sifted

1 teaspoon orange juice

1 teaspoon orange zest

PREPARATION

The Cake

Preheat oven to 350 degrees. Grease a 9x13-inch cake pan or two 9-inch cake pans. Sift flour, baking soda, cinnamon, and salt together; set aside. In a large bowl, beat eggs thoroughly. Add oil, buttermilk, sugar, and vanilla extract and mix well. Add flour mixture, pineapple, carrots, coconut, and pecans. Blend until thoroughly mixed. Pour into prepared pan. Bake 55 minutes or until a wooden toothpick inserted in center comes out clean. While cake is baking, prepare the Buttermilk Glaze.

The Buttermilk Glaze

In a small saucepan, combine sugar, baking soda, buttermilk, butter, and corn syrup. Bring to a boil. Cook 5 minutes, stirring occasionally. Remove from heat and stir in vanilla.

Remove cake from oven and slowly pour glaze over the hot cake. Cool in pan until glaze is totally absorbed.

The Cream Cheese Frosting

Cream butter and cream cheese until fluffy. Add vanilla, confectioner's sugar, orange juice, and orange zest. Mix until smooth.

Frost cooled and glazed cake with the frosting. Refrigerate until frosting is set. This cake may be refrigerated for several days after making.

A Sweet End
to a Winter's Day

A Sweet End to a Winter's Day

Menu

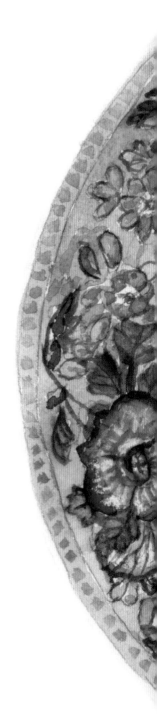

Individual Chocolate Toffee Trifles

Mini Apple Bundt Cakes

Seven Layer Bars

Mini Key Lime Cheesecakes

Sea Salt Caramel Cookies

By the time February arrives, I start to dream about the spring garden, even though I'm still enjoying reading by the fire and the slower pace at the cottage. However, then I think, *Isn't it time for another little gathering? Wouldn't it be nice to invite some neighbors in for a dessert party in front of a roaring fire?* After all, the holiday festivities are fading in our minds, and most everyone is feeling a bit of cabin fever. During this peaceful lull in the year, I have the time to sit down and paint a little invitation for the event.

I suppose my favorite room at Chestnut Cottage is the library. I love this room because it always feels cozy and warm. With thoughts of a dessert party percolating, my mind quickly turned to an antique dessert set I purchased at a recent antique show. I knew it would be perfect for a small gathering in the library, as its color palette is the same.

When I purchased the set, the antique dealer was unsure of the pattern name, only knowing the pieces were stamped "Spode." After a bit of research, I determined the pattern to be "Union Wreath." The color combination in brown and blue displays a center design depicting the English rose, the Scottish thistle, and the Irish shamrock (hence, the "union") with the three repeated in a border in varying shades of blue and brown on a light brown background.

When they're not in use, some pieces of this set hang in the powder room at the cottage.

Recently, I received a gift of "Union Wreath" in blue and white, so now I can be on the hunt for more of this lovely pattern!

With the shapes and pieces in mind, I designed the menu to include some of my favorite desserts. For starters, no good dessert party should be without chocolate, so I chose individual Chocolate Toffee Trifles. I do love supporting local small businesses, so Cold

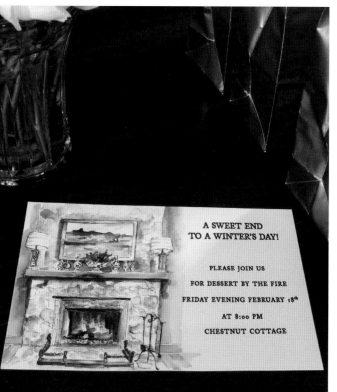

A SWEET END
TO A WINTER'S DAY!

PLEASE JOIN US
FOR DESSERT BY THE FIRE
FRIDAY EVENING FEBRUARY 18th
AT 8:00 PM
CHESTNUT COTTAGE

Mountain Toffee in Waynesville was a perfect source for the toffee. What's more, it also made for a perfect little takeaway gift for guests!

This very rich little dessert should not leave anyone dreaming of more chocolate, but just in case anyone did need (or, rather, want) more chocolate, I decided to make my mother's special recipe for Seven Layer Bars, which include a layer of chocolate. Mother made these bars for many years, and they seem to be a favorite of family and friends.

In an earlier chapter, I shared the recipe for my Fresh Apple Cake. For this party, I decided to make the cake in small individual Bundt pans. No matter how you make it, the cake is always moist and delicious, and the little Bundts fit perfectly in a footed piece of the dessert set.

Thinking this might just be enough chocolate, I added some sea salt caramel cookies and mini key lime cheesecakes to complete the menu.

Afterward, guests lingered by the fire with coffee and conversations of travel to warmer spots before heading out into the chilly February night.

Seven Layer Bars

INGREDIENTS

½ cup unsalted butter, melted

2½ cups graham cracker crumbs

1 cup milk chocolate chips

1 cup butterscotch chips

1 cup shredded, sweetened coconut

1 cup chopped pecans

1 14-ounce can sweetened
    condensed milk

1 teaspoon sea salt

PREPARATION

Preheat oven to 350 degrees. Mix melted butter with the graham cracker crumbs and press in the bottom of a greased 9x13-inch baking pan. Evenly layer the top of the crust with chocolate chips, butterscotch chips, and pecans. Pour condensed milk evenly over the nuts and chips. Sprinkle the coconut in an even layer over the condensed milk and top with salt.

Bake for 25 minutes. Let cool before cutting into bars.

Collecting

Christmas Tree Ornaments

As I said earlier, it is a miracle that Wells indulges my passion for so many Christmas trees and ornaments! There are seven live trees, and I do have one little white artificial tree that was given to me as a gift. It is my only exception to the "all real, fresh trees" rule!

This tree, with a small collection of blue and white ornaments, is tucked into a corner of the keeping room. I have been collecting Christmas ornaments for many years, and each tree represents something of meaning to Wells and me.

Our first Westie, Bentley Greeley, was very demanding and insisted that he have his own tree in the kitchen close to his food and water. This small tree has so many Westie ornaments—and they were passed down to Duncan MacDuff when he came to reside at Chestnut Cottage. Not only is the tree filled with Westie ornaments, but Bentley and Duncan's friends are there too in the form of Goldens, Border Collies, Dalmatians, Scotties, and a neighbor cat. For fun, the tree also holds some of their sworn enemies like squirrels and chipmunks!

Duncan MacDuff often dresses up in his Santa sweater and sits under his tree, hoping to get compliments on just how handsome he is!

The largest tree at the cottage stands in our keeping room. It has a large collection of ornaments, both old and new.

On this tree, my collection includes ornaments from both my grandmother's and mother's trees. Some little porcelain bells my mother purchased in 1952 hang here, along with a snowman made of cotton balls that I made in the first grade. Frosty is missing one arm, but he still manages to sit nicely on the tree.

A Jaguar, a grand piano, and a Kelly bag are a few of my favorite ornaments in the collection, while Wells, of course, prefers his Goldy Gopher.

Goldy Gopher is the mascot at the University of Minnesota, where Wells played college football, so this tree has many Golden Gopher ornaments! A collection of trains (again from my mother) has found a place on this tree.

Each and every ornament brings meaning to the trees, as I know yours do to your tree. I know of no one who doesn't love the ornaments they've collected for their own Christmas tree! Our ornaments evoke memories of Christmas past.

Every time I speak about one particular piece of this collection of trees and ornaments, I think that collection is my favorite. But each tree is truly so unique that I suppose that I can honestly say they are all my favorites!

I am very fond of the tree in our master bedroom that is adorned with ornaments of buildings.

The special position of this tree allows me to sit in bed and see not only it, but also the one beyond in the keeping room. The moment we get up in the morning, we turn on the lights on both trees and enjoy our coffee in bed with each tree twinkling.

A lot of this ornament collection involves travel—the Eiffel Tower, the Leaning Tower of Pisa, Number 10 Downing Street, the Theatre Royal, and many more.

And then there are the beautiful churches, the manger, and so many styles of architecture. I like to give my holiday guests a little tree of their own to enjoy in the guest bedroom, and it always has a garden theme.

Through my years of collecting ornaments, family and friends have given me so many. As I decorate and undecorate the trees, I fondly remember the giver. One of my favorites on this tree is the little beehive with a tiny bee on top. It brings to mind my friend Mary Woltz, the beekeeper based in Sag Harbor, New York, whom you met in an earlier chapter.

Other favorites on the garden tree are Wellingtons filled with gifts, a little greenhouse, and Santa with his watering can.

As you will remember, my maternal grandfather was from Ireland, so both my mother and I had an extensive collection of Irish-themed ornaments. When my mother passed away, my Irish tree had to get substantially larger to hold both her ornaments and mine! The Irish tree stands in the library, my favorite room in the cottage. I spend a lot of time in this room and in my adjoining office, so the placement of this tree was not by accident!

The tree in my cozy little office is done primarily in gold and blue.

Many years ago, my mother crocheted two dozen or so little gold and gold and white bells for this tree.

Along with an assortment of gold angels, I have the Waterford "Twelve Days of

Christmas" and a special golden egg with a tiny copy of *The Collected Tabletop*, made and given to me by my friend Julia Molloy. I'm so lucky that Julia had the patience and talent to craft this little jewel of an ornament!

Wells has his favorite tree, which is in his wine cellar.

This tree started out as a small tabletop tree, but friends continued giving him wine ornaments. As you can see, it is no longer a small tabletop tree that sat on his table in the cellar!

Wells always saves his important corks and has made a garland out of them for this tree.

My favorite of his wine cellar ornament collection is "Blitzen"—down but still holding his bottle and wine glass!

Santa Bacchus sits atop the tree, toasting the holidays.

A table in the wine cellar, with the twinkling tree and surrounded by great bottles of wine, is a lovely venue for an intimate holiday dinner!

I suppose my collection of trees can't expand, as I am out of rooms to put them in at the cottage! But each year, I will lovingly unpack and repack this treasured collection of ornaments and reflect on all the years they have graced so many beautiful, fresh trees.

May all the glories of Christmas past crown each of your Christmases and last through a glad New Year!

Simple Pleasures

PLOTTING NEXT YEAR'S GARDEN

Dreaming of the spring garden while reading through my delightful vintage collection of *My Garden: An Intimate Magazine for Garden Lovers* is a joyful, simple pleasure that the long winter hours provide. I have new plants to consider, orders to place, and designs to finalize!

All this plotting and scheming requires a return to my favorite garden magazine, *The English Garden*; seed and bulb catalogs; and my favorite garden books, which are many!

Many years ago at a client's house, I admired a small set of ivory garden tools in a little wooden caddy. My client fondly remembered where she purchased them in London and told me they had been displayed in her home for many years. Upon her death, her attorney contacted me to let me know that she had left this little set to me in her will. Of course, I was very touched, and now they are on display at Chestnut Cottage. I enjoy having this little set close when I'm plotting the garden.

While at an antique show in Asheville, I purchased a set of thirty-seven leather-bound *My Garden* magazines. My collection spans the years from January 1934 to December 1948 and basically takes up two shelves in the library. If you aren't familiar with them, they are little British magazines filled with garden advice and humorous articles from decades ago.

Not only do these volumes include articles on every imaginable garden subject, but they are also full of unusual, and sometimes amusing, advertisements that often depict the struggles of the war years in England.

"When we are collecting books,
we are collecting happiness."

—VINCENT STARRETT

My Garden includes articles by Constance Spry, suggestions for books for Christmas gifts, tips for planning an herbaceous border, editorials, "did-you-know" lists, poems, letters to the editor, "tulip thoughts," little ink drawings, garden diagrams, a place to make notes, and on and on—truly something to amuse every gardener! These volumes of *My Garden* are so well written that they read more like short novels than a how-to magazine. And the little advertisements in these volumes are so delightful!

Of course, my favorite is Churchill advertising The Royal Cancer Hospital! But I would have found it just as difficult to resist a jolly good biscuit, an arch preserver, or a Waterman pen!

One of my favorite articles, entitled "The Weeding Party," describes an event the writer attended at the home of a Mrs. Pamela Marshall, who, with her family, was celebrating returning to their de-requisitioned house after the war. Before he realized the reason for the invitation, the writer was initially stunned to see that the invitation (written in all capital letters) requested that guests wear their oldest clothes. The hostess thought her idea was grand, since the troops had left her garden in such a state that she was quite ashamed to ask anyone to tea. When guests arrived, they were greeted by Pamela, wearing a dainty flowered apron and pushing a wheeled basket.

The writer, happy to work with his old friend Mr. Marshall, walked around the house where he found people busy everywhere—hacking at briars, stabbing at thistles, and thrashing at nettles with a variety of articles, including walking sticks! A certain Mr. Berwick, a Londoner with no gardening experience who had come to the country after his flat in London was bombed, joined the rest. The once lovely garden had become a wilderness, and the Marshalls' friends were accepting the weeding challenge with spirit. There were to be prizes for the most weeds pulled (over which animated disagreements ensued even among the children). It was also known that the Marshalls were planning to serve ham ("filleted ones in a tin from America") to their guests when the work was done.

After hours of work, the author edged towards the house (and the ham!), when he heard slow steps approaching from behind. It was Mr. Berwick, dragging an overflowing box towards the terrace steps. Mr. Berwick indicated that he could hardly tear himself away from the garden work and never dreamed it could be so fascinating. "I found yards and yards of this stuff, the ground was almost solid with it, but I think I've got every inch of it out for you, Mrs. Marshall," he cheerfully reported.

Proudly, he laid at her feet her famous and long-established lily-of-the-valley bed—the source of inspiration for a soon-to-be much-anticipated and highly regarded annual party that she had hosted before the war!

What fills your quiet winter hours in front of a warm fire? I believe we should all make time for our simple pleasures.

O ur time together is coming to a close. What a treat it has been to have you at Chestnut Cottage for this year-long journey. Gardening, collecting, and hosting family and friends are what makes our house a home, and it is one of my greatest joys to share it with you.

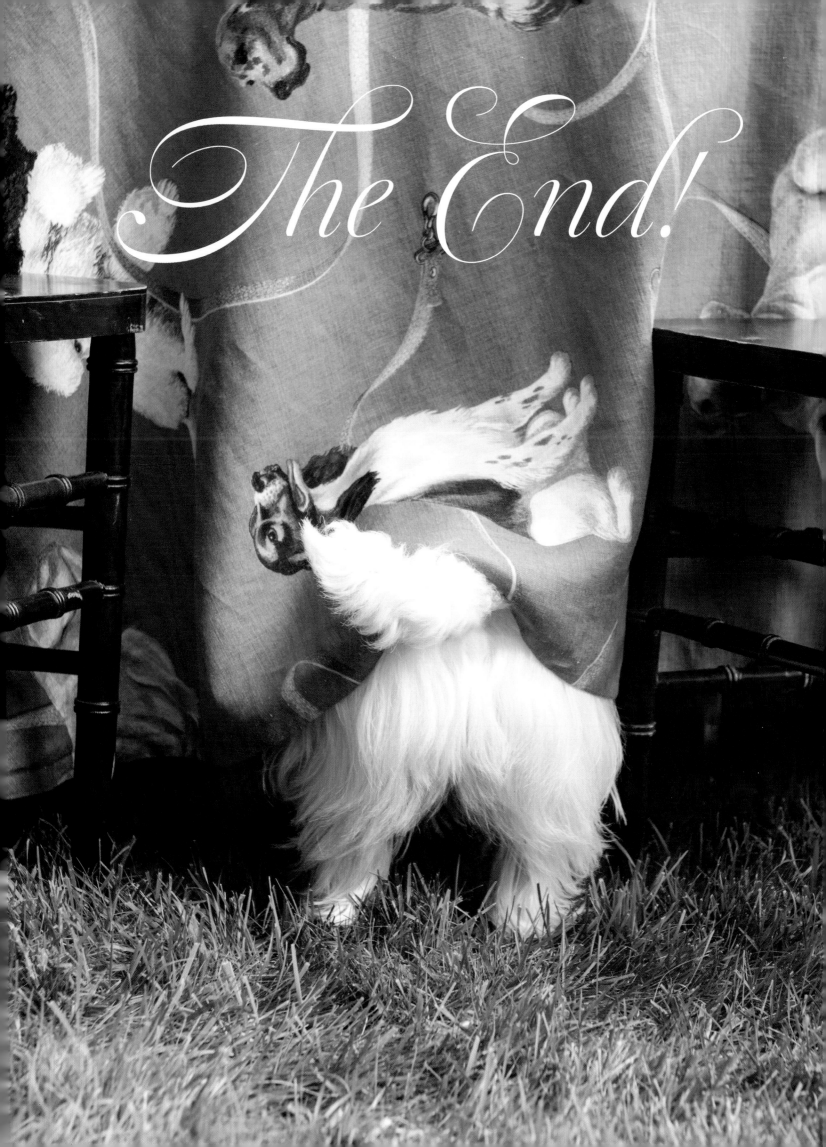

The End!

Acknowledgments

At Kathryn Greeley Designs, we believe that every project takes a team to be successful. Both this book and *The Collected Tabletop* were no exception to this belief. In working on *The Collected Cottage*, I certainly had the "A-Team." Once again, my photographer, J. Weiland, gave this project his full attention, even during the challenges of a pandemic. J. gave me his best work, his patience (and he needed lots of this!), his great sense of humor, and his great photographic ability. We have laughed throughout this project, agreeing that being twelve years older made this book harder than when we did *The Collected Tabletop*! Thank you, J., for standing by me and making the dream of *The Collected Cottage* come true.

Two other important players on this A-Team are my husband, Wells, and my friend/housekeeper, Margie Carver. Wells has been unfailing in his support and excitement for this project. Wells never said no to any crazy thing I asked him to do, and he did so with love, patience, and good humor when the cottage was turned upside down, with buckets of flowers everywhere, and the kitchen looking like a total wreck! Margie has been my "right-hand person" for every photo shoot, working tirelessly to keep everything in order and Chestnut Cottage sparkling. I could not have done this book without Wells and Margie, and I thank them both from the bottom of my heart.

A very special thanks to Jenny Luczak of Green Truck Gardens for all of her hard work and expert advice in the garden.

Thank you, Tiffany Adams, for blessing my thoughts after I finally got them on paper. And thank you to my Design Assistant, Janice Feichter, for keeping everything running smoothly at Kathryn Greeley Designs while I worked on this book.

When I started *The Collected Tabletop*, my dear friend Ed Springs lovingly volunteered to paint all of the lovely watercolor menus. When I shared with Ed that I wanted to do another book, he again graciously offered to do any artwork that I might desire for *The Collected Cottage*. Ed started with the incredible hand drawing of the cottage and its grounds. I had envisioned this book would be divided into the four seasons, and Ed said he would be happy to do drawings of areas around Chestnut Cottage that would represent the four seasons. Ed indicated he would watercolor the drawings and would be happy to paint anything else I might want to show in the book. Together, Ed and I thought it would be great to use each china pattern I use in the book in some fashion. Ed finished the drawing of the seasons but sadly passed away of cancer before he was able to watercolor the seasons or do any of the china patterns. My heart was broken to lose Ed, my dear friend of so many years. I strongly believe that when God closes one door, He always opens another. When I shared my sadness with my friend and client Margaret Roberts, who is also an artist, Margaret immediately said she would like to watercolor Ed's season drawings and paint the china patterns. How can one person be so blessed to have the support of these two friends and talented artists? As Margaret painted each season drawing and each china pattern, I became more and more delighted and grateful for her immense talent. So, thank you, Margaret, for all you have done for this book!

Thank you to Replacements for their generosity and continued support. A special thanks to Julie Robbins at Replacements for her research and help for locating treasures that I needed for gatherings and collections. So much of my china, crystal, and silver collections have come from Replacements, and working with them through the years has brought me much joy!

I am surrounded by so many talented people and would like to thank Emily Followill and Sandra Stambaugh for their contributions of images, and a special thanks to my friend Maria West for my personal images.

So many antique dealers have assisted me through my many years of collecting, and I am grateful for their help and inspiration. Two dealers have assisted me in both this book and my first book. Village Antiques in Asheville, North Carolina, and Vivianne Metzger Antiques in Cashiers, North Carolina—thank you both for your continued support!

A special thanks also to Blossoms Creative and LTM Designs for their careful assistance and attention to details with invitations, place cards, and menu cards, and for their tasteful creativity. And to Catherine Langsdorf for her lovely calligraphy.

A special thanks to my friend Annette Anderson, who was my constant sounding board for this book, helped in the kitchen, and was always there to render her sage advice. Thank you to all of my friends and clients who have supported me with unwavering love and faith.

And thank you, James Farmer, for being so much fun and for your kind words in the foreword!

Last but certainly not least, I want to thank my team at Greenleaf Book Group. A special thanks to Tanya Hall, CEO of Greenleaf, for her continued support and belief in me; my editor Sally Garland, who constantly inspired me; Chase Quarterman, for his lovely book design; Tyler LeBleu, who kept this entire project on schedule; and to everyone else at Greenleaf who worked behind the scenes.

I finish this book with a very grateful heart for all of this unbelievable help!